MORE RECIPES
FROM A KITCHEN GARDEN

MORE RECIPES
FROM A KITCHEN GARDEN

Renee Shepherd and Fran Raboff

Ten Speed Press
Berkeley, California

Copyright © 1995 by Renee Shepherd

All rights reserved. No part of this book may be reproduced in any form without the written permission of the publisher, except in the case of brief quotations embodied in critical articles or reviews.

🔟

Ten Speed Press
P.O. Box 7123
Berkeley, CA 94707

Cover design by Linda Lane and Marianne Ackerman
Text design by Linda Lane and Marianne Ackerman

Library of Congress Cataloging-in-Publication Data
Shepherd, Renee.
More recipes from a kitchen garden / Renee Shepherd and Fran Raboff.
    p.   cm.
    Includes index.
    ISBN 0-89815-730-7
    1. Cookery (Vegetables) I. Raboff, Fran. II Title.
TX801. $48 1995
641.6'5—dc20   94-47272
                                                CIP

FIRST PRINTING 1995
Printed in the United States
1 2 3 4 5—99 98 97 96 95

Dedication

To Al Raboff.
A perfect gentleman who knows
how to live life with joy, love, and style.

CONTENTS

ACKNOWLEDGMENTS

Mimi Osborne's marvelous illustrations reflect both her talent and her horticultural expertise and make this book a pleasure for everyone who uses it, including its authors.

Linda Lane's graphic creativity and skill in design combine perfectly with her care and good judgment in all our joint projects.

Glenna von Gease's ability to take my handwritten scrawl on yellow pads and turn it into crisply typed, well organized work never fails to amaze me. She is a true friend who never says "too late," "too much," or "not now," and is a blessing in my life.

Beth Benjamin, coworker and close friend, calms me when I'm ruffled, inspires me when I'm down, and her gentle spirit keeps me dedicated in all the ways that count, both personally and professionally.

David Pearce kept the house and garden running smoothly while this cookbook was in progress and gave careful critical feedback on recipes in progress. Although he has moved into an office role now, he still keeps the blues and black holes in my life at bay and reminds me that music, laughter, and loyal friendship are essential ingredients.

Bill Arnold has been a valued friend and recipe evaluator whose unswerving interest and support, sense of humor, and quiet, solid presence have come to my rescue time after time, helping to bring coherency and calm to an otherwise hectic schedule of responsibilities.

Wendy Krupnick's constant horticultural stewardship and love make the gardens flourish, and her conscientious attention to detail has made this cookbook come together much more easily.

Trevor, Melissa, and Matthew Boynton are the children in my life who help me remember how to play in the garden and see the joy and beauty in everyday things.

WHY COOK FROM THE GARDEN

Every time Fran and I begin a cooking session, I think of the extra advantage we kitchen gardeners have because using fresh vegetables and herbs makes a tremendous difference in the process and rewards of everyday cooking. It is a much different experience for all the senses to cook with a basket of just-picked sweet peppers and chiles in a rainbow of hues that look like a still life portrait, or to have a big bouquet of fragrant basil or citrusy lemon thyme still smelling like the sun in front of you when you pull out a pan and take chopping knife in hand. The process of cooking with the fruits of one's own labor adds another dimension to creating good meals. Even if you don't have a garden of your own, supermarkets all over the country have expanded their produce sections remarkably in the last decade, and the welcome advent of local farmers markets has greatly increased every cook's access to a wide range of freshly picked ingredients.

Americans have come of age in the last decade when it comes to good food. We have begun to celebrate our tremendous geographical and ethnic diversity for its ability to enrich our food choices. We relish our own regional dishes and explore the influences and ingredients of the many other cultures available to us. Southwestern, Indian, Japanese, Caribbean, Northwestern, Szechuan, Mexican, Thai, Vietnamese, healthy Mediterranean—all these trends of recent years, and many more, have opened up new realms of ingredients and ideas. We have become comfortable with a new sense of the "center of the plate," that is, the heightened importance and presence of vegetables, grains and legumes in all our meals, combining healthfulness with good taste. This new focus on the quality and quantity of vegetables in cooking really comes together best in the gardener's kitchen, where we can grow an extraordinarily diverse variety of food to experiment with and learn from, and play with every day.

Cooking from the garden also gives us a real sense of the seasonality of our environment as we harvest each crop at the peak of its flavor and quality. Finally, and perhaps most importantly, the kitchen garden gives connection to the earth and demonstrates how we are part of natural cycles as both stewards of our environment, and it's beneficiaries. For me, cooking with the fruits of my own garden labor is a very real, practical sacrament that can be practiced and celebrated each day.

How Our Garden Grows

Originally, I began writing recipes to go in the catalog of the gourmet vegetable seed company I began in 1984. Joining forces with Fran greatly expanded my horizons and productivity, and we now create dozens of recipes each year to help customers find fresh ideas for using their harvests. We try to keep in mind that, like ourselves, the readers of both our cookbooks and seed catalog, want delicious, easy-to-prepare dishes that emphasize flavor and health conscious technique, and maximize simplicity and appetizing presentation.

We do recipes each season for every kind of vegetable and herb, realizing, for example, that if you grow cilantro for the first time, you'll need ideas on how to enjoy it after making fresh salsa becomes routine. If you have an especially abundant crop of sorrel or basil, you'll want good ideas on how to take advantage of it beyond the one or two standard recipes that come easily to mind. When your bean or potato harvest comes all at once, good dishes to expand your everyday repertoire are a godsend. And naturally we work hard to offer memorable solutions to the problem of an endless supply of tomatoes or summer squash, so they remain a delight and not an embarrassment of riches!

Our own gardens are in two locations at my home, which is on 4 acres in the hills of Santa Cruz, California. The original garden is in my backyard, laid out in long raised beds and managed with classic French intensive organic techniques. We try to build our soil and tilth constantly, and plant crops to come in and out throughout the gardening year. Here we grow all manner of leafy vegetables, a cornucopia of salads and root vegetables, brassicas from all nations, peas and heirloom potatoes, annual and perennial herbs, and edible flowers. The 1/2-acre lower garden is located below the house in an old converted horse pasture. After cover cropping to increase fertility and humus content each winter, it is laid out in spring in raised wide rows and drip irrigated. Here we grow all the fruiting vegetables such as melons, squash, cucumbers, pumpkins, eggplants, tomatoes in all their forms and colors, lots of rainbow peppers, and my newest love, chiles— from mild to fiery hot. Both gardens serve as living catalogs for visitors who come to see our varieties and how we grow them. Master gardener Wendy Krupnick, who plants and manages the gardens, interplants our crops both with plants that attract beneficial insects and with many wonderful flowers for bouquets, everlastings, and fragrance flowers.

In addition to harvesting for the kitchen, we use the gardens to evaluate new varieties. For example, one year we'll grow fifteen different Thai chiles to see which we favor; the next season it may be twelve new cherry tomatoes in different colors or ten Piel de Sapo Spanish melons to see which tastes best and keeps longest. Lately we've been growing chiles from Thailand, Mexico, Chile, Belize, and Africa, and experimenting with unusual salad greens such as orach and edible amaranth.

THE RECIPE PROCESS

Each week Fran and I plan out new recipes depending on what is available to harvest. We come up with recipes in a myriad of ways: Seed company customers generously share their favorites and we collect cooking magazine articles, talk to chef friends, and look at every food publication we can. Often it is a process of thinking of how the flavor of one ingredient may go with another. We may see a recipe for broccoli and think about how it would be if we made it with cauliflower instead and perhaps added lemon and ginger. Sometimes we take a recipe we already know and change it with new aromatics. Doing recipes with specialties like scented geraniums is especially challenging and fun because there isn't much literature on the subject and we often just taste a leaf and think about what we could combine it with!

Next we rough out recipes and plan a menu. Twice a week throughout the garden year we get together in Fran's commodious kitchen. Fran shops for basic ingredients and I arrive with a basket of the needed produce and herbs picked that day. We prepare everything and begin to cook, often improvising and creating new flavor combinations in the process. When everything is ready, we set the table, open the wine, and sit down for our tasting meal with Al, Fran's husband, and our invited friends. I keep the penciled recipes next to me at the table and we get everyone's reactions and suggestions. We often change things at this stage, as one of us suggests an addition or modification—for example, more or less garlic, adding chopped dried tomatoes or scallions, or using another kind of cheese. There are always a number of successes as well as a few dishes that don't pan out, but we always learn (knowing what doesn't work is sometimes just as valuable as knowing what does). The next stage is the seemingly endless process of retesting and refining the recipes, and finally writing them up in clear, understandable terms (which is quite a lot harder than it seems). Then we make the completed recipes once again to be certain everything is just right.

FINALLY

In completing this new cookbook, Fran and I have consciously worked to create recipes lower in saturated fat with an emphasis on healthy everyday eating. Both of us think this really isn't much of a chore, for when you are focusing on beautiful fresh vegetables and herbs, their essential flavors are so delicious that a cook really doesn't need added embellishment like rich sauces. All of these recipes have been thoroughly tested and enjoyed over the last four years by our families and circle of friends at happy and memorable meals, both in my kitchen and in Fran's wonderful dining room overlooking the redwood-covered mountainside. We invite you to share them with pleasure, satisfaction, and friendship. Please do send us your feedback and ideas because these shared conversations are always important sources of the inspiration and fellowship that all gardeners and cooks need to continue to grow and flourish. Enjoy!

VEGETABLES

GRILLED VEGETABLES

*Barbecuing vegetables brings out their sweetness and
imparts a smoky, nutty quality that is extraordinarily delicious.
Once you try this, you'll do it as often as you're inclined
to light up the coals all harvest season.*

❖

*Choose colorful, ripe, garden-fresh vegetables, such as
summer squash, eggplants, onions, and different colored bell
peppers. Cut eggplant, onions and squash on the bias into about
½-inch thick slices. Cut peppers into 2- to 3-inch strips or big
scallops. About an hour or so before cooking, combine vegetables
with any good olive oil-based vinaigrette, or use balsamic
vinegar and olive oil with added minced garlic and basil, pepper
and salt. Prepare a barbecue fire, preferably using fruit wood or
mesquite chips. When coals are evenly at the white ash stage,
drain vegetables well and grill on a fine mesh barbecue grid
about 4 to 6 inches from the coals. Grill as slowly as possible
until tender when pierced, turning several times and
moving vegetables around with a fork so they cook evenly.
(A little charring on the edges doesn't hurt them.)
Enjoy warm with or without a meat course,
and have crusty French bread to
sop up the tasty juices.*

ARTICHOKES

LEMON- AND PARSLEY-STUFFED BAKED ARTICHOKES

This recipe's simple two-step cooking process results in an unparalleled tenderness while the parsley-lemon stuffing brings out the artichokes nutty flavor.

4 medium artichokes
4 tablespoons lemon juice
3 cups chopped parsley
1 tablespoon chopped fresh sage
2 cloves garlic, minced
zest of 1 lemon, grated
½ teaspoon salt
¼ teaspoon freshly ground pepper
3 tablespoons olive oil
1 onion, thinly sliced

✤ Preheat oven to 350°F. Discard the stems and rough outer leaves of the artichokes and trim tops. Parboil in a large pot of lightly salted water for 15 minutes. Drain upside down; cool. Spread the artichoke leaves apart gently. Using a small spoon, scrape out the fuzzy inedible (choke) part of the artichokes. Sprinkle inside with 2 tablespoons of lemon juice. Combine parsley, sage, garlic, lemon zest, salt and pepper. Spoon this mixture into the center and between leaves of each artichoke.

Mix together olive oil and remaining 2 tablespoons lemon juice and set aside. Arrange the onion slices in the bottom of a deep baking dish just large enough to hold the artichokes snugly. Arrange artichokes right side up, side by side in dish on top of onions. Drizzle with the olive oil and lemon juice mixture. Add boiling water to the bottom of the pan to a depth of 1 inch. Cover tightly with foil. Bake artichokes for 1 to 1 ¼ hours, basting occasionally with pan juices. Serve hot or at room temperature.

Serves 4

ITALIAN STUFFED ARTICHOKES

These delicious and elegant stuffed artichokes are a wonderful first course or perfect luncheon dish for a special occasion. We had it first on a balcony overlooking the Mediterranean on the island of Capri. The chef who shared it with us spoke no English, so we worked the recipe out in ragged but earnest French over the course of a perfect afternoon of food talk.

4 large artichokes
½ lemon

FILLING:
2 cups finely diced tomatoes, well drained
1 cup (3 ounces) finely diced
*   mozzarella cheese*
½ cup (3 ounces) thinly sliced prosciutto
½ cup chopped fresh basil

VINAIGRETTE DRESSING:
1 large clove garlic, minced
1 large shallot, minced
1 scallion, finely chopped
2 tablespoons lemon juice
¼ cup olive oil
freshly ground pepper to taste

GARNISH:
Mayonnaise

❧ Cut off stems and discard small outer leaves at the base of each artichoke. With a scissors cut off sharp thorns on leaves. Trim about 1 inch from tops. Rub cut surfaces with lemon. Steam artichokes for 45 to 50 minutes until the outer leaves are tender. Let cool. Spread the leaves apart gently. Pull out center choke leaves, then with a small spoon or melon ball scoop carefully scrape out the fuzzy inedible choke.

In a bowl combine filling ingredients. In a separate bowl, combine all vinaigrette ingredients except oil. Slowly whisk in oil, beating until well blended. Pour dressing over filling mixture and toss until combined. Gently spread artichoke leaves apart. Spoon some of the filling into center and around leaves. Arrange on lettuce lined plates. Serve with mayonnaise if desired.

Serves 4

Asparagus

Asparagus and Mushroom Risotto

A very satisfying traditional favorite, lightened up for summer enjoyment.

1 pound asparagus, trimmed
3 tablespoons olive oil
½ pound mushrooms, trimmed and
   halved
1 shallot, finely chopped
1 medium to large onion, chopped
1 cup Arborio rice or other short-grain
   white rice
½ cup dry white wine
3 to 3 ½ cups chicken broth
½ cup freshly grated Parmesan or Asiago
   cheese
salt and pepper to taste
2 tablespoons chopped parsley

✤ Slice asparagus into ½-inch pieces. If the stems are very thick, slice them lengthwise in half. In a large skillet, heat 1 tablespoon of the oil, add asparagus and mushrooms, and sauté, stirring, until vegetables are tender-crisp. Remove from pan and set aside.

Add the remaining 2 tablespoons of oil, shallot, and onion to the skillet and sauté 2 or 3 minutes, until shallot and onion are softened. Over low heat, add rice, stirring for 2 minutes until rice is coated. Add wine and 3 cups of broth. Bring to a boil. Cook uncovered over medium low heat, stirring often, until rice is almost tender, about 15 to 20 minutes.

Reduce heat and stir frequently until mixture has a creamy consistency, about 5 minutes. Add asparagus and mushrooms. Cook for 4 to 5 more minutes. If rice is not quite tender, add an additional ½ cup of broth. If rice is too wet, raise the heat until liquid is absorbed. Stir in half of the cheese, add salt and pepper. Sprinkle parsley and remaining cheese over the top. Serve immediately.

Serves 4 to 6

COLD ASPARAGUS WITH SESAME-GINGER VINAIGRETTE

A simple but elegant marriage of ginger and sesame with poached asparagus.

1 pound asparagus, trimmed

DRESSING:
1 tablespoon toasted sesame seeds
  (see recipe)
1 small clove garlic
1 teaspoon grated fresh ginger
2 tablespoons rice vinegar
2 tablespoons orange juice
2 teaspoons soy sauce
2 tablespoons vegetable oil
1 teaspoon sugar
¼ teaspoon red chile flakes
¼ teaspoon sesame oil

❋ Bring lightly salted water to a boil in a medium skillet, add asparagus, and cook until just tender-crisp, about 5 minutes. Immerse asparagus in ice water to stop the cooking. Pat dry and arrange on a platter. Chill. Just before serving, mix together the dressing ingredients and pour evenly over asparagus. Serve on a platter.

Serves 4

ASPARAGUS AND MUSHROOMS WITH ORANGE SAUCE

Fresh sweet asparagus, earthy mushrooms, crunchy green onions, and a hint of orange flavor a light spring feast.

1 pound asparagus
1 tablespoon olive oil
1 tablespoon butter
1 clove garlic or 1 shallot, minced
3 scallions, white part only, sliced thin
  (reserve tops for garnish)
2 cups sliced mushrooms
salt and freshly ground pepper to taste

ORANGE SAUCE:
grated zest of ½ medium orange
3 tablespoons orange juice
3 tablespoons white wine
1 teaspoon cornstarch

GARNISH:
¼ cup sliced scallion tops

❋ Combine ingredients for orange sauce and reserve.
  Trim asparagus and cut into 1-inch lengths. (If asparagus stalks are large, cut in half lengthwise.) In a medium skillet heat the oil and butter. Add garlic and scallions and sauté until softened, about 3 to 4 minutes. Add asparagus and sauté 2 minutes. Add mushrooms and sauté, stirring constantly, another 3 minutes. Add orange sauce to vegetables, cooking and stirring until mixture thickens, about 1 to 2 minutes. Add salt and pepper to taste. Transfer to serving bowl, sprinkle scallion tops over the asparagus, and serve immediately.

Serves 4

ASPARAGUS FRITTATA

*A handsome and flavorful brunch or lunch dish that really sets off
fresh home-grown asparagus.*

¾ pound asparagus, trimmed
salt and pepper to taste
2 tablespoons olive oil
1 ¼ cups (4 ounces) sliced fresh
   mushrooms
3 scallions, sliced
6 eggs, lightly beaten
3 tablespoons milk
1 tablespoon chopped parsley
1 teaspoon chopped fresh basil
½ teaspoon chopped fresh thyme
1 tablespoon butter
¼ cup freshly grated Parmesan cheese
¼ cup grated Fontina or Mozzarella
   cheese
2 tablespoons crunchy bread crumbs (or
   crush French bread crusts)

❊ Preheat oven to 450°F.

Cut asparagus stalks into 1-inch pieces; you should have about 3 cups. Steam covered in water until barely tender. Drain and season with salt and pepper. Set aside.

In a large heavy ovenproof skillet, heat 1 tablespoon olive oil over medium heat. Add mushrooms and scallions and sauté until softened. Remove from skillet and reserve. Drain off excess liquid.

Beat eggs lightly with milk. Stir in parsley, basil, thyme, salt, and pepper.

To the skillet add remaining 1 tablespoon olive oil and butter and heat until foamy. Pour in egg mixture and cook over low heat until eggs are cooked on the bottom but still soft on top. Remove from heat. Arrange asparagus and mushroom mixture over eggs. Sprinkle over cheese and bread crumbs. Place skillet on upper rack of the oven and bake just until top is firm and cheese has melted. Do not overcook.

Serves 6

ASPARAGUS SOUFFLÉ

Light, subtle, fluffy, and delicious—a great way to enjoy fresh asparagus.

2 teaspoons soft butter
3 tablespoons freshly grated Parmesan cheese
1 ⅓ cups chopped, cooked asparagus, cooled and drained
2 large egg yolks (reserve whites)
1 tablespoon flour
⅓ cup grated Swiss cheese
½ cup low fat sour cream
1 teaspoon Dijon mustard
⅛ teaspoon salt
¼ teaspoon pepper
large pinch nutmeg
2 tablespoons chopped parsley
4 egg whites, at room temperature
¼ teaspoon cream of tartar

❄ Preheat oven to 375°F. Spread butter inside 6 individual custard cups or a 6-cup soufflé dish. Sprinkle inside of dishes with half of the Parmesan cheese. In a blender or food processor combine asparagus, egg yolks, flour, Swiss cheese, sour cream, mustard, salt, pepper, nutmeg, and parsley. Process or blend until mixture is puréed. Remove to a large bowl. In another bowl beat egg whites until foamy. Add cream of tartar and continue beating until stiff but not dry. Quickly and gently fold egg whites into asparagus mixture. Spoon into prepared custard cups or soufflé dish, mounding the mixture higher in the center. Sprinkle top with remaining Parmesan cheese. Bake 30 to 40 minutes (depending on size of dish) until soufflé is golden brown on top and a skewer inserted in the center comes out clean. Serve immediately.

Serves 4

Beans

Green Beans with Olives

A slightly offbeat but delicious combination that we enjoyed throughout the green bean season this year.

1 pound green beans
1 tablespoon butter
1 tablespoon olive oil
1 small clove garlic, minced
2 scallions, finely chopped
½ cup sliced pimento-stuffed green olives
1 ½ tablespoons lemon juice
salt and pepper to taste

✤ Cook beans in a large pot of boiling salted water until just tender-crisp, 3 to 5 minutes. Drain beans in a colander and plunge immediately into ice water to stop the cooking. Drain and cut into 1-inch pieces. Set aside.

Heat butter and olive oil in a large skillet. Add garlic and scallions and sauté until softened. Add beans, olives, and lemon juice and sauté until heated through. Add salt and pepper to taste. Serve immediately.

Serves 4

Joanna's Green Beans

With caramelized onions and sautéed peppers, this green bean dish tastes rich and looks beautiful.

1 tablespoon butter
3 tablespoons olive oil
½ medium onion, very finely chopped
2 red bell peppers, julienned
3 tablespoons chicken broth or bouillon
1 tablespoon lemon juice
1 pound green beans, trimmed
salt to taste

✤ In a large skillet, melt butter, add 2 tablespoons of the oil, and heat gently. Add onion and red pepper and sauté slowly over medium low heat until peppers are tender-crisp and onion is translucent and tender. Remove half of this mixture and reserve. Add last tablespoon of the oil to the pepper and onion mixture remaining in the skillet. Continue to sauté over low heat for 4 to 5 more minutes until onions are very soft and beginning to caramelize. Add the chicken broth and lemon juice, put mixture into food processor or blender, and process until creamy. Steam green beans until tender and drain. Combine the green beans, the reserved sautéed pepper and onion, and the onion/pepper purée. Salt to taste. Heat through and serve.

Serves 4

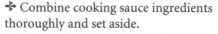

STIR-FRY GREEN BEANS WITH PORK,
ONION AND TOMATOES

A fast and satisfying main dish that uses green beans' fresh flavor to best advantage.

COOKING SAUCE:
1 tablespoon soy sauce
1 teaspoon sugar
1 tablespoon dry sherry
1 teaspoon red wine vinegar
¼ cup chicken stock

1 pound green beans
3 tablespoons peanut oil
2 cloves garlic, minced
1 tablespoon minced fresh ginger root
1 onion, thinly sliced and separated into
   rings
½ pound lean ground pork
2 tomatoes, seeded and cut into sixths
2 teaspoons cornstarch dissolved in
   1 tablespoon water

GARNISH:
3 scallions, thinly sliced

❖ Combine cooking sauce ingredients thoroughly and set aside.

Prepare beans by cutting them diagonally into 1-inch lengths. Heat a wok or large skillet and add 2 tablespoons of the oil. Add green beans and stir-fry for 3 to 4 minutes. Remove beans with a slotted spoon and set aside. Add 1 more tablespoon of oil to wok; add garlic, ginger, and onion and stir-fry for 30 seconds just until vegetables are fragrant. Add pork and cook, stirring frequently, until pork is no longer pink. Add tomatoes and green beans, stir-frying for 2 minutes, just until beans are just tender-crisp. Pour in cooking sauce mixture and cook, stirring, for 1 minute. Add dissolved cornstarch, stirring until sauce thickens. Top with scallions and serve with rice.

Serves 4 to 6

PACIFIC RIM GREEN BEANS

East meets West and both approve!

*1 pound green beans, trimmed and cut
  in half*
1 tablespoon butter or margarine
1 tablespoon oil
1 clove garlic, minced
1 red onion, chopped
2 tablespoons chopped red bell pepper
1 serrano chile pepper, seeded and minced
1 teaspoon grated fresh ginger
¾ cup chicken stock
2 teaspoons soy sauce

✤ In a medium saucepan heat butter
and oil over medium heat. Add garlic,
onion, red pepper, chile pepper, and
ginger and sauté until all ingredients
are softened. Add string beans, tossing
until coated. Stir in chicken stock and
soy sauce. Cover and cook over moderate heat until beans are tender-crisp.

Serves 4 to 6

GREEN BEAN SALAD WITH WALNUT DILL DRESSING

*Garden fresh green beans with a creamy
dill dressing set off by crunchy nuts.*

1 pound green beans, trimmed

SALAD DRESSING:
½ cup chopped red onions
¼ cup chopped Italian parsley
⅓ cup chopped fresh dill
3 tablespoons white wine vinegar
¼ cup chopped toasted walnuts
⅓ cup olive or walnut oil
2 tablespoons plain low fat yogurt
2 tablespoons low fat sour cream

GARNISH:
Chopped toasted walnuts

✤ Bring a large pot of salted water to a
rolling boil, add green beans and cook
until just tender-crisp, 3 to 5 minutes.
Refresh beans with ice water to stop the
cooking, drain, pat dry, and refrigerate.
In a blender or food processor, combine dressing ingredients, blending
until smooth. Serve beans on lettuce
leaves. Spoon dressing over beans.
Sprinkle with nuts before serving.

Serves 4 (makes 1 cup dressing)

LIME GREEN BEANS

Fresh lime juice and zest are perfect partners for tender green beans in this delicate sauté.

**1 pound green beans, trimmed
  and halved
1 tablespoon butter
1 teaspoon sesame oil
1 clove garlic, minced
grated zest of 1 lime
1 tablespoon fresh lime juice
salt and freshly ground pepper to taste**

✣ Steam or cook green beans until just tender-crisp. In a small skillet heat butter and sesame oil. Add garlic and sauté until fragrant. Add lime zest and juice and beans, tossing until combined. Add salt and pepper to taste. Serve immediately.

Serves 4 to 6

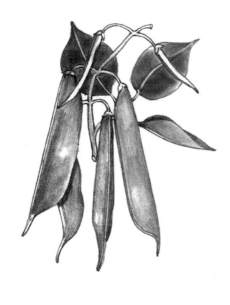

ATHENIAN PLAKA SALAD

Beautiful to look at and delicious to eat, the hearty flavor of this traditional Mediterranean salad is a real crowd pleaser.

1 pound fresh green beans, ends trimmed

DRESSING:
**3 tablespoons white wine vinegar
1 tablespoon lemon juice
1 clove garlic, minced
4 scallions, finely chopped (white part
  only—chop tops and reserve for garnish)
⅓ cup finely chopped fresh mint leaves
⅓ cup chopped fresh Greek basil
1 tablespoon chopped fresh oregano
⅓ cup olive oil
salt and freshly ground pepper to taste
½ cup crumbled feta cheese
½ cup toasted slivered almonds
2 hard-boiled eggs, chopped fine**

GARNISH:
Reserved scallion tops

✣ Combine dressing ingredients well and reserve. Bring a large pot of lightly salted water to a boil. Put in green beans and cook until just tender-crisp, about 3 to 5 minutes. Drain beans in a colander and plunge immediately into ice water to stop cooking action. Drain on paper towels. Mix dressing thoroughly with beans. Arrange beans in a pinwheel fashion on a large platter. Mound crumbled feta in center of platter, and surround with nuts and chopped eggs, and sprinkle reserved scallion tops over all.

Serves 4

FLAGEOLET BEAN GRATINÉE

In the French tradition, a savory and satisfying main dish casserole, high in both flavor and nutrition. A great Sunday-at-home dish to make on a cold wet day.

1 ½ cup dried green flageolet beans, soaked overnight in water to cover by at least 3 inches, then drained
2 tablespoons olive oil
2 cloves garlic, minced; 3 if you like garlic a lot
1 onion, finely chopped
1 carrot, diced
1 stalk celery, diced
2 teaspoons chopped fresh thyme
¼ cup chopped fresh parsley
1 bay leaf
5 cups chicken broth
3 medium tomatoes, seeded and diced
¼ cup chopped fresh basil

TOPPING:
1 cup bread crumbs mixed with
  3 tablespoons freshly grated Parmesan
  or Asiago cheese
2 tablespoons olive oil

❧ Preheat oven to 350°F. Heat 2 tablespoons oil in 5- to 6-quart pot. Add garlic, onions, carrot, and celery and sauté until softened, 5 to 7 minutes. Add thyme, parsley, bay leaf, chicken broth, and beans. Bring to boil, cover and simmer for about 45 minutes or until beans are almost tender. Simmer uncovered for another 30 minutes until the liquid is reduced but still just covers the beans. The juices should thicken slightly. Remove bay leaf. Add tomatoes and basil. Spoon into an 8 x 11-inch baking dish. Spread crumb topping mixture over casserole and drizzle with the remaining 2 tablespoons of olive oil. Bake 30 to 35 minutes or until bubbly.

Serves 4 to 6

CARIBBEAN BLACK BEAN SOUP

A wonderful soup with lively rich flavor and smooth hearty texture.

2 to 3 tablespoons olive oil
2 large onions, chopped
3 cloves garlic, chopped
3 stalks celery, with leaves, chopped
1 pound (about 2 ½ cups) dried black
  beans, soaked overnight in water to
  cover by at least three inches, then
  drained
1 ½ to 2 pounds ham hocks or ham shank
10 cups chicken stock
½ teaspoon dried cayenne pepper
1 ½ teaspoons cumin
2 tablespoons balsamic vinegar
¼ cup dry sherry
salt and freshly ground pepper to taste

GARNISHES:
low fat sour cream, chopped hard boiled
  eggs, chopped scallions, and cilantro

❧ In a large soup pot, heat oil and add onion, garlic, and celery. Sauté until vegetables are softened. Rinse soaked beans and add them to the pot along with the ham hocks and chicken stock. Bring to a boil, reduce heat, add cayenne and cumin. Partially cover the pot and simmer over low heat for 2 ½ to 3 hours, or until beans are soft, stirring occasionally. Remove ham hocks and let cool. Skim excess fat from soup, then purée soup in batches in a food processor or blender. Return bean purée to soup pot. If desired, cut ham meat from bones in small pieces and add to soup.

Bring soup to a simmer over low heat and just before serving, add vinegar, sherry, salt, and pepper to taste. Serve hot with a dollop of sour cream surrounded by chopped egg, scallions, and cilantro.

Serves 10

BEETS

FRESH BEET HORSERADISH

This wine-red horseradish is especially good served with fresh yogurt over beet greens, chard, or baked potatoes.

2 ½ cups (about ½ pound) peeled and
 diced horseradish root
¼ cup mild red wine vinegar
½ cup rice vinegar
2 small beets, cooked and peeled
½ teaspoon salt, or to taste
2 to 3 tablespoons sugar, or to taste

❧ In a food processor, process horse-radish and vinegars until horseradish is finely ground. Add beets, salt, and 2 tablespoons of sugar and process until combined. Add more sugar and salt, if needed. Place in a glass jar and refrigerate.

Makes 2 cups

 Note: Without a food processor, finely grate horseradish and beets and combine with vinegar, salt, and sugar.

BRITT'S BEET AND GREEN APPLE SALAD

A crisp and absolutely beautiful salad that came to us from a wonderful young friend who cooks from the garden for twelve hungry organic farmers every day!

5 to 6 medium to large beets (about
 1 ½ pounds)
½ small red onion, chopped
2 tart green apples, cut in halves, cored
 and thinly sliced (unpeeled)

DRESSING:
1 shallot, minced
1 teaspoon Dijon mustard
1 teaspoon horseradish
1 ½ tablespoons red wine vinegar
¼ teaspoon celery seed
2 tablespoons vegetable oil
2 tablespoons olive oil
¼ teaspoon salt
freshly ground pepper to taste

GARNISH:
⅓ cup chopped scallions
2 tablespoons chopped fresh dill

❧ Wash beets, but do not peel. Cook in water to cover until tender when pierced with a sharp knife. Cool, peel, and cut in half, then slice halves into thin slices. Place beets in a salad bowl with onion and apple slices. Combine dressing ingredients and toss with salad. Garnish with scallions and dill, and serve.

Serves 6 to 8

Beets with Raspberry-Mint Vinaigrette

The earthy sweet beets are perfectly highlighted by a light fruity dressing.

1 ½ pounds unpeeled beets (about 6 medium)
2 large shallots, minced
3 tablespoons raspberry vinegar
1 tablespoon lemon juice
1 tablespoon grated orange zest
4 scallions, finely chopped
2 tablespoons chopped fresh mint leaves
¼ cup olive oil
salt and pepper
1 lime

✿ Steam beets until tender. Cool, peel, and cut into ¼-inch slices. In a mixing bowl combine shallots, vinegar, lemon juice, orange zest, scallions, and mint. Whisk in olive oil, mixing until emulsified. Add beet slices and toss until coated. Add salt and pepper to taste. Squeeze lime juice over the beets and toss lightly. Serve warm.

Serves 4 to 6

Rosy Beet/ Napa Cabbage Slaw

A crunchy sweet/sour rosy slaw that is hard to beat when hot weather potlucks beckon you and your family. Plan to bring the recipe!

6 cups thinly sliced Napa or regular cabbage leaves
1 ½ cups chopped red onion
2 medium beets, grated
1 cup chopped fresh parsley
¼ cup red wine vinegar
½ cup water
2 tablespoons brown sugar
½ teaspoon salt
⅓ cup chopped fresh dill leaf
3 tablespoons chopped fresh chives
½ cup low fat sour cream
salt and freshly ground pepper

✿ Combine vegetables and parsley in a large bowl. In a saucepan, combine vinegar, water, sugar, and salt. Bring to a boil, stirring until sugar is dissolved. Pour over vegetables and toss. Add dill and chives and mix in well. Cover and let marinate overnight. Stir well once or twice. Just before serving, drain off excess liquid. Stir in sour cream and add salt and pepper to taste.

Serves 4 to 6

BROCCOLI

BROCCOLI WITH REMOULADE SAUCE

Garden fresh broccoli paired with a classic savory sauce.

1 large bunch broccoli (about 1 ½ pounds)

REMOULADE SAUCE:
1 tablespoon wine vinegar
2 teaspoons Dijon mustard
1 tablespoon capers, drained
⅛ teaspoon sugar
1 teaspoon chopped fresh tarragon
2 tablespoons finely chopped scallions
2 tablespoons low fat mayonnaise
⅓ cup low fat sour cream

GARNISH:
2 tablespoons chopped chives

✤ Remove and discard coarse leaves of broccoli. Cut off the tough bottoms of the stalks. Peel the stems and split the large ones in half lengthwise. Steam the broccoli, or cook covered in several inches of lightly salted boiling water until just tender-crisp. Drain and transfer to a serving platter. Thoroughly combine Remoulade sauce ingredients and pour sauce over broccoli. Garnish with chives and serve.

Serves 4 to 6

MARINATED BROCCOLI STEMS

Crispy, flavorful, low calorie finger food.

Stems from 4 or 5 large broccoli stalks
* (about 1 pound)*
2 tablespoons rice vinegar
1 ½ tablespoons sugar
½ teaspoon salt
1 tablespoon chopped fresh tarragon
1 teaspoon sesame oil
sesame seeds, toasted

✤ Peel broccoli stems; cut into ⅛ to ¼-inch slices. In a bowl or large jar, combine vinegar, sugar, salt, and tarragon, stirring until sugar dissolves. Add broccoli stems, stirring to coat thoroughly. Cover and refrigerate overnight, stirring once or twice. Before serving, drain off liquid and mix in sesame oil. Sprinkle with sesame seeds.

Serves 4

SIRIMA'S BROCCOLI AND SHRIMP SALAD

Beautiful colors and crunchy textures highlight this great marriage of flavors.

1 pound broccoli
2 scallions, thinly sliced
½ red bell pepper, julienned
½ to ¾ pound cooked small shrimp

DRESSING:
¼ cup rice vinegar
1 ½ tablespoons sugar
½ teaspoon salt
½ teaspoon finely chopped fresh ginger
2 tablespoons vegetable oil
½ teaspoon sesame oil
freshly ground pepper to taste

GARNISH:
2 tablespoons toasted sesame seeds

❧ Cut the broccoli florets from their stems and separate into small clusters. Peel the stems and cut into julienne strips. Bring 2 quarts of lightly salted water to a boil. Add broccoli florets and stems and cook until just tender-crisp, about 2 minutes. Drain and plunge into ice water. When chilled, drain thoroughly and put into a bowl. Add scallions, bell pepper, and shrimp.

Combine all dressing ingredients, whisking in oil until well blended. Toss with broccoli and marinate for 1 to 2 hours. Just before serving, sprinkle with sesame seeds.

Serves 4 to 6

FRESH BROCCOLI SOUP

A very light and subtle-tasting soup to showcase garden-ripe broccoli. Good hot or chilled.

1 ½ pounds broccoli—a large bunch
2 tablespoons olive oil
2 cloves garlic, chopped
1 medium to large onion, chopped
2 tablespoons lemon juice
½ teaspoon chopped fresh thyme
    or lemon thyme
½ teaspoon salt
¼ teaspoon pepper
boiling water
2 cups chicken stock
1 cup whole milk
½ teaspoon nutmeg

GARNISH:
2 tablespoons chopped chives

❧ Cut the tops of the broccoli into florets. Peel the stems and cut into ¼-inch slices. In a saucepan, heat oil, add garlic, onions, and broccoli, and sauté until onions are slightly softened. Add lemon juice, thyme, salt, and pepper. Cover with 2 inches of boiling water. Cover pan and cook until tender. Purée in blender with chicken stock. Return to saucepan, add milk and nutmeg and heat through but do not boil. Taste for seasoning. Garnish with chopped chives.

Serves 6

Green in Snow Stir Fry

The sesame flavors complement this tempting vegetable stir fry which includes no onion or garlic, making it very easy on sensitive stomachs.

3 tablespoons sherry
3 tablespoons soy sauce
1 teaspoon finely chopped fresh ginger
¾ cup chicken stock
3 tablespoons vegetable oil
1 medium cauliflower — cut into florets
1 medium head broccoli — cut into florets
¼ cup toasted sesame seeds
1 teaspoon sesame oil
1 ½ tablespoon cornstarch dissolved in 2 tablespoons water

✤ Make sauce by combining sherry, soy sauce, ginger, and chicken stock. Heat the oil in a wok or large skillet. Stir-fry the vegetables for 3 to 4 minutes. Add sauce and sesame seeds, mixing together well. Cover and steam/cook another 3 to 4 minutes, or until just tender-crisp. Uncover and sprinkle sesame oil over vegetables. Stir in cornstarch mixture and cook about 1 minute more or until sauce thickens. Serve immediately.

Serves 6

Broccoli Salad with Tarragon Dressing

Broccoli's crunch and tarragon's punch seem just made for each other in this sprightly salad, which is one of my favorites for potlucks.

2 bunches broccoli, trimmed and cut into florets with 2-inch stalks

SALAD DRESSING:
1 clove garlic, minced
2 tablespoons white wine vinegar
2 tablespoons sweet pickle relish
2 tablespoons chopped parsley
2 tablespoons chopped chives
2 tablespoons chopped fresh tarragon
¼ teaspoon salt
freshly ground pepper to taste
⅓ cup olive oil

GARNISH:
6 to 8 large lettuce leaves
petals of 5 or 6 calendula flowers

✤ Bring a large pot of salted water to a rolling boil. Add broccoli florets and cook just until tender-crisp, about 3 to 4 minutes. Refresh broccoli with ice water to stop the cooking. Drain, pat dry, and refrigerate until serving. Combine dressing ingredients, whisking in oil gradually until well blended. Arrange broccoli on lettuce leaves. Pour dressing over. Garnish with calendula petals.

Serve 4 to 6

BRUSSELS SPROUTS

NORTH COAST BRUSSELS SPROUTS

A great dish we first dreamed up from the north coast of Santa Cruz, California, where Brussels sprouts are a primary specialty crop.

1 pound Brussels sprouts, trimmed
2 cups chicken stock
1 tablespoon butter or margarine
2 tablespoons olive oil
1 pound mushrooms, sliced
2 shallots or 3 scallions, chopped
salt and pepper to taste

❋ Place Brussels sprouts in a saucepan with the chicken stock, cover and cook until just tender, then drain and keep warm. In a heavy skillet, heat butter and oil, add mushrooms and shallots (or scallions), and sauté slowly until vegetables are softened. Add Brussels sprouts and heat through. Add salt and pepper to taste.

Serves 4

DILL BRAISED BRUSSELS SPROUTS

A new favorite for enjoying sprouts' sweet crispness.

1 pound fresh Brussels sprouts
2 tablespoons olive oil
½ teaspoon salt
¼ teaspoon fresh ground pepper
3 tablespoons chopped fresh dill leaf
⅓ cup water
2 tablespoons fresh lemon juice
1 to 2 teaspoons butter
3 tablespoons grated Parmesan cheese

❋ Trim outer leaves if necessary, then slice off ends of Brussels sprouts. Cut into 3 or 4 slices or if small, cut in half. Heat oil in a skillet, add sprouts and stir fry until coated with oil and bright green. Add salt, pepper, dill, water, and lemon juice; cover and cook 2 minutes or until tender but still crunchy. Toss with butter and Parmesan cheese.

Serves 4

BRUSSELS SPROUTS WITH
APPLE CIDER AND LEMON THYME

*The nutty, sweet flavor of garden fresh Brussels sprouts is
perfectly complemented by this lemony piquant sauce.*

1 tablespoon butter
2 teaspoons olive oil
1 large shallot, minced
1 medium onion, finely chopped
2 tablespoons chopped sundried tomatoes
1 pound Brussels sprouts, trimmed and
  halved
¾ cup apple cider
¾ cup water
1 tablespoon chopped lemon thyme
2 tablespoons fresh lemon juice
salt and pepper to taste

❖ In a medium skillet, heat butter and oil, add shallot, onions, and sundried tomatoes and sauté until softened. Add Brussels sprouts and cook for 3 minutes longer, stirring. Add apple cider and water. Bring to a boil, reduce heat, cover and simmer for 10 to 15 minutes, or until Brussels sprouts are tender. With a slotted spoon remove Brussels sprouts to a warm serving dish. Cook liquid in skillet over medium-high heat until it is reduced by half. Add lemon thyme and lemon juice and cook, stirring, for 1 more minute. Pour sauce over Brussels sprouts. Add salt and pepper to taste.

Serves 4

CABBAGE

NAPA CABBAGE MAGYAR

*Tastes rich—but isn't! This new stuffed cabbage dish is very satisfying and hearty fare.
Serve with crusty bread to mop up the sauce. Great as leftovers too!*

16 to 18 large Napa cabbage outer leaves

STUFFING:
5 to 6 turkey sausages (about 1 pound),
  casings removed
1 bunch scallions, chopped
½ cup chopped parsley
1 cup fresh bread crumbs (2 slices whole
  grain bread)
¼ cup chicken stock
1 teaspoon Worcestershire sauce
2 egg whites

SAUCE:
2 tablespoons olive oil
1 onion, finely chopped
1 cup crushed tomatoes
¾ to 1 cup chicken stock
¾ cup red wine
3 tablespoons vinegar or lemon juice
1 teaspoon chopped fresh thyme
2 tablespoons sugar
6 gingersnaps, crumbled

GARNISH:
⅓ cup low fat sour cream

✣ In a large pot of boiling salted water, blanch cabbage leaves 3 at a time for 3 to 4 minutes, or until slightly softened. Drain cabbage, pat dry. With a sharp knife, trim out the thick vein of each leaf to make it lie flat. To stuff cabbage, arrange leaves vein side down and place a rounded tablespoon of stuffing near base of each leaf. Roll up folding in sides of leaf to enclose filling.

In a 4- or 5-quart saucepan, heat oil, add onion and sauté until softened. Add tomatoes, chicken stock, wine, vinegar or lemon juice, thyme, and sugar, stirring until combined. Place cabbage rolls in sauce. Bring to a boil, then cover, reduce heat and gently simmer for about 50 minutes, until filling is cooked through. With a slotted spoon transfer cabbage rolls to a warm platter. Skim off any excess fat from remaining sauce. Add crumbled gingersnaps to the sauce, and cook, stirring, over low heat until mixture thickens. Return cabbage rolls to pan and baste with sauce, or spoon sauce over cabbage rolls on a warm platter. Top with sour cream and serve.

Serves 6 to 8

BONNIE'S CABBAGE CUCAMONGA

A meatless casserole that is delicious the first day and also makes great leftovers. Good potluck dish too!

5 to 6 large potatoes, boiled and made into mashed potatoes; use butter, milk, salt and pepper to your taste.
1 tablespoon each, olive oil and butter
2 large cloves garlic, finely chopped
1 small head red cabbage, shredded thinly
freshly ground pepper
2 cups shredded medium Cheddar cheese
2 ounces crumbled feta cheese
1 tablespoon sweet paprika

❧ Preheat oven to 350°F. In a large skillet, heat oil and butter, add garlic and sauté just until fragrant. Add shredded cabbage and sauté until just wilted, not soft. Stir in lots of freshly ground pepper.

Spread mashed potatoes in a lightly greased 9 x 12-inch baking dish. Cover with sautéed cabbage and Cheddar cheese, then sprinkle over feta and top with paprika. Bake 20 to 25 minutes until hot and cheese has melted.

Serves 6 to 8

PAK CHOI KIMCHEE

A gardener's version of the classic Korean pickle. This is a very habit forming dish—great for refrigerator raids!

1 pound pak choi
2 cloves garlic, minced
3 small slices fresh ginger root
½ teaspoon chile flakes
1 scallion, cut into 2-inch lengths
1 tablespoon soy sauce
1 teaspoon rice vinegar
1 teaspoon salt
2 teaspoons sugar

❧ Cut enough pak choi to make 3 cups into 1-inch lengths, using mostly the stalks.

Combine garlic with ginger, chile flakes, scallion, soy sauce, and vinegar. Add the pak choi and mix well with your hands. Add salt and sugar, mixing again until well combined. Let stand for 1 to 2 hours at room temperature as it will make its own juice, then refrigerate until ready to serve.

Makes 1 pint

CRYSTAL CITY PAK CHOI

A stir-fry with a Japanese twist that features the clean, crisp sweetness of pak choi with a savory sauce and sesame garnish.

2 bunches Pak choi
(approximately 1 ½ pounds)
2 tablespoons olive oil
1 clove garlic, minced
1 red onion, thinly sliced
1 teaspoon dry mustard
1 tablespoon soy sauce
1 teaspoon rice vinegar
1 tablespoon sake or dry sherry
3 scallions, finely chopped
2 tablespoons finely chopped parsley
salt and freshly ground pepper to taste

GARNISH:
2 tablespoons toasted sesame seeds

Cut Pak choi stalks into 1-inch lengths. Shred green tops and reserve. In a large skillet, heat oil, add garlic and onions and stir fry until softened. Stir in Pak choi stalks, mustard, and soy sauce and stir fry until Pak choi is tender, about 10 to 12 minutes. Stir in shredded tops, vinegar, sake or sherry, scallions, parsley, and salt and pepper to taste. Cover and cook 2 more minutes. Garnish with toasted sesame seeds and serve immediately.

Serves 6

HEATHER'S FRESH MINESTRONE SOUP

Our friend Heather's active family loves this "meal in a pot"—her garden yields all the fresh ingredients for this satisfying dish that falls somewhere between a soup and a stew. It is even better when flavors are allowed to blend for a day before serving. A traditional favorite to serve with fresh crusty bread and green salad.

4 slices meaty bacon
1 large or 2 medium onions, chopped
6 large cloves of garlic, minced
2 large carrots, chopped
3 cups shredded cabbage
one 14 ounce can red kidney beans
2 medium zucchini, chopped
6 cups chicken stock
2 tablespoons tomato paste
½ small hot chile, minced, or ¼ teaspoon
   red pepper flakes
¼ cup chopped fresh parsley
1 tablespoon chopped fresh oregano
1 teaspoon chopped fresh thyme or
   lemon thyme
½ cup chopped fresh basil
1 large red, yellow, or orange bell pepper,
   chopped
8 large ripe plum tomatoes
1 cup broccoli florets
1 cup cauliflower florets
4 cups shredded spinach or chard
one 8-ounce package of fresh pasta
   (not dried) cut into 2-inch lengths
salt and freshly ground pepper to taste

GARNISH:
freshly grated Parmesan or Asiago cheese

✢ In a heavy skillet, fry bacon until crisp, then remove from pan, drain, and finely chop. Discard all but 3 tablespoons of the bacon drippings. Add the onion and garlic to the bacon drippings in the skillet and sauté slowly until limp and translucent, about 4 to 6 minutes. Transfer onion mixture and reserved chopped bacon to a large heavy soup pot, then add all remaining ingredients except pasta. Bring to a boil, then reduce heat and simmer for 1 hour. Add the pasta the last 3 minutes of cooking. When soup is done, add salt and lots of freshly ground pepper to taste. Serve hot, passing freshly grated cheese at the table to top each bowl.

Serves 8 to 10

SOLIDARITY CASSEROLE

Serve with beer or ale and dark bread. A meal in itself for a blustery cold fall day—but not too heavy, so it won't weigh you down!

3 medium red potatoes
2 tablespoons vegetable or olive oil
1 medium onion, chopped
1 teaspoon fresh summer savory
½ cup chopped red or green pepper
2 sweet apples, cubed
2 ½ teaspoons crushed mustard seeds
5 cups shredded cabbage
¾ pound low-fat Kielbasa sausage, sliced
   ½-inch thick
1 pound jar sauerkraut, drained
⅓ cup chicken broth
2 ½ tablespoons brown sugar
freshly ground pepper to taste
2 tablespoons chopped parsley

❊ Preheat oven to 350°F. Parboil potatoes in boiling water for 12 minutes, then drain and cut into ¼-inch slices and reserve. In a large skillet, heat oil and add onions, savory, peppers, apples, and mustard seeds. Sauté until vegetables and fruit are softened. Add cabbage and sausage, stirring until cabbage is wilted. Add reserved potato slices, sauerkraut, chicken broth, sugar, ground pepper to taste, and parsley. Simmer uncovered for 5 minutes then put mixture in a casserole, cover, and bake for 1 hour.

Serves 8

CARROTS

SIRIMA'S SPECIAL THAI CARROT SALAD

This salad combines sweet, sour, hot, and pungent—all the classic flavor dimensions in every mouthful.

4 cups coarsely shredded carrots
¾ cup halved cherry tomatoes, slightly crushed
*⅞ ounce (standard package) dried, coarsely ground or chopped shrimp, crumbled
2 teaspoons minced garlic
2 serrano or other very hot chile peppers, seeded and finely chopped (use 1 for mild heat; 2 for moderate; 3 to 4 for fiery)
3 tablespoons freshly squeezed lime juice (reserve rinds)
*2 tablespoons bottled fish sauce
1 ½ tablespoons sugar

✤ In a bowl, combine carrots, tomatoes, ground dried shrimp, garlic, and chile peppers. Add lime juice, fish sauce, and sugar. Add 3 or 4 of the squeezed lime rinds to the salad to enhance flavor; cover and marinate in the refrigerator for at least 2 hours so the lime shells leave a faint lime peel flavor and other flavors combine and mature. To serve; sprinkle over chopped cilantro. Traditionally a spoonful of salad is wrapped in a fresh lettuce leaf to eat like a burrito.

*Dried shrimp and fish sauce or Naam Pla are available in the Oriental Section of most good markets.

Serves 6 to 8

JULIA'S CARROT TZIMMES

A wonderful dish from the Jewish holiday tradition that works beautifully as a side dish for roast chicken, lamb, or turkey.

1 cup chicken stock
⅓ cup orange juice
2 tablespoons lemon juice
2 tablespoons dark brown sugar
3 tablespoons honey
½ teaspoon cinnamon
dash nutmeg
2 tablespoons butter
5 carrots, peeled, cut diagonally into 1-inch slices
3 sweet potatoes, peeled, cut into 1-inch slices
½ pound pitted prunes

✤ Preheat oven to 375°F. Lightly grease an 8 x 11-inch shallow baking dish. In a saucepan combine chicken stock, orange and lemon juices, sugar, honey, cinnamon, nutmeg, and butter. Bring to a boil, reduce heat, and simmer for 2 to 3 minutes.

Arrange carrots, sweet potatoes, and prunes in the baking dish. Pour the hot stock mixture over them, turning them once in the mixture. Cover and bake 1 hour or until vegetables and prunes are tender. Uncover and baste frequently until carrots and sweet potatoes are golden brown on top.

Serves 4 to 6

FIRE ISLAND CARROTS

This dish is a Thanksgiving tradition in the Rhode Island family of our graphic designer, who made it for our annual postcatalog celebration last year.

1 pound carrots, peeled and cut into
*   1-inch chunks*
1 clove garlic, finely chopped
1 stalk celery, finely chopped
1 ½ cups chicken stock (approximately)
1 teaspoon chopped fresh thyme
1 tablespoon red wine vinegar
⅛ teaspoon red pepper flakes
¼ teaspoon ground cumin
2 teaspoons butter
¼ cup chopped parsley
salt to taste

✲ In a saucepan, combine carrots, garlic, and celery and add enough chicken stock to cover. Bring to a boil, cover, and simmer until carrots are barely tender. Uncover and add thyme, vinegar, red pepper flakes, and cumin and boil rapidly until about ¼ cup liquid remains. Add butter and parsley. Salt to taste.

Serves 4

GLAZED CARROTS WITH MINT SAUCE

The bright flavors of fresh carrot and mint are perfectly married in this dish.

1 pound carrots, sliced thin
2 tablespoons butter or margarine
1 teaspoon lemon juice
1 ½ tablespoons sugar
⅓ cup chicken stock
salt and freshly ground pepper to taste
2 teaspoons chopped fresh mint

✲ In a small saucepan, steam carrots over boiling water until just tender-crisp. Drain. Heat butter in a deep skillet. Add carrots, lemon juice, and sugar. Cook over medium heat, shaking the pan until carrots are coated. Add chicken stock and continue cooking slowly until liquid is evaporated and carrots are light golden. Add salt and pepper to taste. Add mint and mix in well. Serve immediately.

Serves 4

MAPLE AND ORANGE GLAZED CARROTS

Maple, fresh thyme, ginger, and orange combine to make a fruity tasting herbed glaze for fresh carrots.

1 tablespoon butter
2 teaspoons grated fresh ginger
1 bunch scallions, chopped (reserve 2 tablespoons of green part for garnish)
1 pound carrots, peeled and sliced into ¼-inch rounds
2 teaspoons grated orange zest
1 cup orange juice
3 tablespoons maple syrup
1 tablespoon chopped fresh lemon thyme leaves
salt and freshly ground pepper to taste

GARNISH:
Reserved scallion tops

✣ In a medium saucepan, melt butter. Add ginger and the white part of scallions and sauté for 1 minute. Add carrots, orange zest, and juice. Cover pan, bring to a boil, then reduce heat and simmer until carrots are just tender, about 12 to 15 minutes. Add maple syrup and lemon thyme and cook uncovered, stirring frequently until the liquid becomes syrupy, about 5 minutes. Add salt and pepper to taste. Garnish with chopped scallion tops.

Serves 4

CURRIED CARROT SLAW

Carrots, peanuts and a creamy curry dressing combine perfectly in this fresh pretty vegetable slaw/salad.

3 cups shredded carrots
½ cup golden raisins
3 tablespoons thinly sliced scallions, including part of the green
6 slices bacon, cooked until crisp, crumbled
½ cup roasted peanuts

DRESSING: combine well:
¼ cup low fat mayonnaise
¼ cup low fat sour cream
1 teaspoon sugar
½ teaspoon curry powder

GARNISH:
Fresh orange slices, skin and pith removed

✣ In a bowl toss together the carrots, raisins, and scallions. Mix in bacon and peanuts, then add dressing, tossing to thoroughly coat. Serve immediately, garnishing with orange slices.

Serves 6

MARMALADE CARROT SQUARES

Rich carrot bars with a hint of chocolate.
Best if made a day in advance to let flavors blend.

butter
1 teaspoon cocoa powder
¾ cup flour
½ teaspoon baking powder
½ teaspoon baking soda
¼ teaspoon ground cloves
½ teaspoon allspice
½ teaspoon cinnamon
½ teaspoon salt
2 eggs at room temperature
½ cup sugar
1 ½ cups finely grated carrots
½ cup orange marmalade
½ cup grated semisweet chocolate
½ cup ground walnuts

GLAZE:
1 cup powdered sugar, sifted
2 tablespoons orange juice
1 tablespoon grated orange zest

❖ Preheat oven to 350°F. Thoroughly grease a 9 x 9-inch baking pan with butter. Sprinkle with cocoa and set aside. Sift together flour, baking powder, baking soda, cloves, allspice, cinnamon, and salt. In a mixing bowl beat eggs until thick and lemon colored. Add sugar, mixing well. Mix in carrots, marmalade, chocolate, and walnuts. Fold in dry ingredients, mixing until combined. Spoon batter into baking pan. Bake 40 to 45 minutes until cake tester inserted in center comes out clean.

Glaze: Combine powdered sugar, orange juice, and orange zest until mixture is a spreadable consistency. Spread onto warm cake. Cut into squares before serving.

Makes 12 servings

Caramelized Vegetable Soup Stock

For those who prefer a meatless all-purpose stock, this recipe produces a flavorful broth good on its own or as a basis for any number of dishes. Freeze it in ice cubes to add as a flavor enhancer to almost any savory dish.

3 tablespoons olive oil
3 large cloves garlic, peeled and halved
2 large onions, peeled and quartered
3 large leeks, white part only, chopped (reserve green leek tops)
4 large carrots, peeled and cut into chunks
3 large stalks celery, cut into 3-inch pieces (reserve leaves for broth)
1 small turnip, peeled and cut into chunks
10 cups water
1 cup coarsely chopped parsley, including stems
¼ cup coarsely chopped fresh thyme, including stems
1 bay leaf
¼ teaspoon peppercorns
¼ teaspoon allspice
2 slices fresh ginger, cut into ⅛-inch thick slices
salt and freshly ground pepper to taste

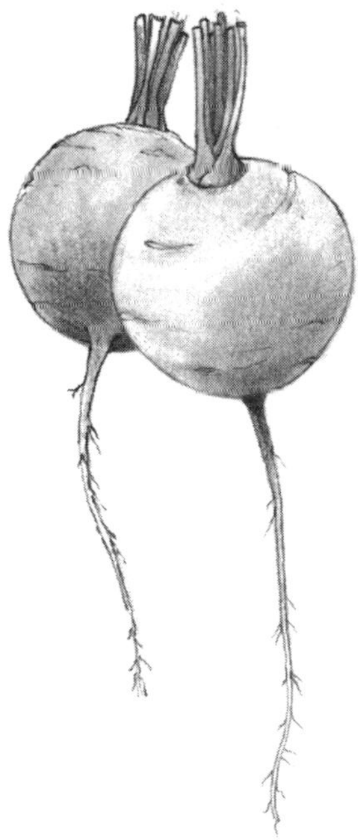

In a large heavy bottomed soup pot or Dutch oven, heat 2 tablespoons of the oil. Add garlic, onions, leeks, carrots, celery, and turnip and sauté at a very low heat, stirring frequently, for 50 to 60 minutes until vegetables are golden and slightly caramelized. Add water and the remaining herbs and spices and reserved celery leaves. Cover the stock entirely with the reserved green leek tops. Bring to a boil, reduce heat, and simmer for 1½ hours. Strain the stock into a bowl through a sieve or colander, pressing firmly on the solids to extract as much of the liquid as possible, then discard vegetables. Add salt and pepper to taste to the broth. Cool and refrigerate or freeze.

Makes 8 cups

CAULIFLOWER

CAULIFLOWER WALDORF SALAD

In an unusual twist on the traditional Waldorf, the mild and faintly nutty flavor of crunchy garden-fresh cauliflower is enhanced with apples, blue cheese, and nuts.

½ teaspoon salt
1 clove garlic, minced
¼ cup red wine vinegar
1 tablespoon lemon juice
2 teaspoons chopped fresh lemon thyme
½ cup mild olive oil
freshly ground black pepper to taste
4 cups cauliflower flowerets, cut into small pieces
1 cup chopped celery
3 red apples, unpeeled and diced, or cut into thin slices
1 small onion, very finely chopped
1 cup chopped fresh parsley

GARNISH:
3 chopped scallions
½ cup crumbed blue cheese
¾ cup pecans, toasted and chopped

❊ Sprinkle the bottom of a large salad bowl with salt. Rub garlic into the salt with the back of a spoon. Add vinegar, lemon juice, and thyme. Gradually whisk in the olive oil until well blended. Add pepper to taste. Mix in cauliflower, celery, apples, onion, and parsley. Marinate for several hours.

Just before serving, lightly mix in scallions and blue cheese, and top with pecans.

Serves 8

CAULIFLOWER AND BABY PEA SALAD

This salad is light and pretty as a picture; with the ham and a crusty bread it makes a fine meal.

1 medium cauliflower, cut into medium-size florets
2 cups fresh or defrosted baby peas
¼ cup chicken stock
2 stalks celery, finely chopped
3 scallions, finely chopped
2 tablespoons chopped parsley
⅓ cup chopped red bell pepper
1 tablespoon balsamic vinegar
1 tablespoon Dijon mustard
3 tablespoons low fat sour cream
⅓ teaspoon each salt and white pepper
1 cup cooked chopped ham (optional)

GARNISH:
chopped chives

❊ Steam cauliflower and peas just until barely tender. Drain well and put into a bowl. Add the chicken stock and set aside to cool. Combine celery, scallions, parsley, red bell pepper, vinegar, and mustard. Mix in sour cream and add salt and pepper. Toss gently with cauliflower and peas, adding ham if desired. Sprinkle with chives and serve.

Serves 6

CAULIFLOWER-BRIE SOUP

A rich-tasting and sumptuous soup that will help make a cook's reputation.

1 large cauliflower (1 ½ to 2 pounds)
1 tablespoon butter or margarine
1 tablespoon olive oil
2 cloves garlic, minced
3 cups coarsely chopped onion
4 cups chicken stock
3 tablespoons unconverted white rice
1 tablespoon lemon juice
1 cup low fat milk
⅛ teaspoon cayenne pepper
½ teaspoon freshly grated nutmeg
3 tablespoons chopped chives
3 ounces Brie cheese
salt and white pepper to taste

GARNISH:
Reserved cauliflower florets
1 tablespoon vegetable oil
Parmesan cheese
1 tablespoon chopped chives
paprika

✢ Core cauliflower and cut into florets (approximately 6 cups)—reserve a few florets for garnish. In a large saucepan, heat butter and oil and sauté garlic and onion until softened. Add cauliflower, chicken stock, and rice. Bring to a boil, then reduce heat and simmer for 20 to 25 minutes until cauliflower is very tender. Remove from heat. Stir in lemon juice. Purée mixture in a food processor or blender, then return mixture to saucepan. Heat slowly, stir in milk, cayenne, nutmeg, and 2 table-spoons of chives and cook, stirring constantly, until soup is hot. Cut off outside of Brie cheese if it is crusty and hard. Cut cheese into small chunks and add to soup, stirring until it is slightly melted. Add salt and white pepper to taste.

To serve: While soup is heating, sauté reserved florets in the 1 table-spoon of oil until slightly softened. Roll florets in Parmesan cheese, drop in soup. Sprinkle with remaining 1 tablespoon of chopped chives and paprika before serving.

Serves 6-8

CAULIFLOWER CARROT SOUP

A satisfying low fat summer meal in a pot. Perfect with a green salad and crusty bread.

1 tablespoon butter or margarine
1 tablespoon olive oil
2 cloves garlic, minced
1 large onion, chopped
2 large carrots, thinly sliced
1 cauliflower (about 1 ½ pounds), broken
   into florets
½ cup dry sherry
3 ½ cups chicken stock
¼ cup chopped parsley
1 cup low-fat or regular milk
¼ teaspoon nutmeg
salt and freshly ground pepper to taste

GARNISH:
½ fresh lime
2 tablespoons chopped chives

✤ In a 4- to 5-quart saucepan, heat butter or margarine and oil. Add garlic and onion and sauté until softened, about 3 to 4 minutes. Add carrots, cauliflower, and sherry; heat and stir together for 3 minutes longer. Add chicken stock. Bring to a boil, reduce heat, cover and simmer 30 to 35 minutes or until vegetables are tender. Add parsley. Purée in a blender or food processor. Return mixture to saucepan. Add milk and nutmeg, and salt and pepper to taste. Heat, stirring, until completely hot, but do not allow to boil. Squeeze juice of ½ lime over soup. Before serving, garnish with chives.

Serves 6

Celeriac

Celeriac with Creamy Mustard Dressing

The dressing brings out the complex nutty-sweet flavor of celeriac. Serve hot or cold.

DRESSING:
2 tablespoons finely chopped parsley
2 tablespoons Dijon mustard
1 tablespoon sugar
3 tablespoons sour cream mixed with 3
   tablespoons fresh plain yogurt
   (or use all sour cream)
1 large or 2 small knobs celeriac

✤ Reserving one tablespoon of the parsley, combine all the other dressing ingredients well and set aside in refrigerator to blend flavors. Scrub celeriac and cut away tough root fibers. Cook whole in boiling salted water until tender when pierced with a fork, about 25 to 30 minutes. Drain celeriac. When cool enough to handle, cut off outer skin and carefully slice into ½-inch-thick cubes or slices. Arrange on a serving dish and spoon dressing over. Sprinkle reserved tablespoon of chopped parsley over the top and serve.

Serves 4

Celeriac Slaw

A fine appetizer or salad course.

3 cups peeled celeriac, shredded or cut into
   julienne (match stick) strips
1 tablespoon fresh lemon juice
1 tablespoon herb salad dressing—okay to
   use a bottled dressing
2 tablespoons mayonnaise
2 tablespoons good-quality Dijon mustard
1 ½ tablespoons chopped fresh chives
1 ½ tablespoons chopped fresh parsley

✤ Sprinkle celeriac strips with lemon juice and mix. Combine with all other ingredients and mix well. Refrigerate for at least one hour before serving, as the dressing tenderizes the celeriac and mingles the flavors.

Serves 5 to 6

CELERIAC AND SLICED TOMATO SALAD

A fine appetizer or salad course in the traditional European fashion.
Nice heaped in fresh, hollowed out tomato halves.

2 to 3 small, firm celery roots, about
   1 pound

DRESSING:
2 tablespoons lemon juice
1 tablespoon white wine vinegar
1 teaspoon Dijon mustard
dash Worcestershire sauce
2 tablespoons chopped parsley
2 scallions, thinly sliced
¼ cup olive oil

TO SERVE:
lettuce leaves
2 or 3 tomatoes, cut into ¼-inch slices
3 tablespoons chopped chives
1 hard-cooked egg, chopped

✢ Scrub and peel celery roots. Boil in water to cover or steam until tender when pierced with a knife, about 40 to 45 minutes. Drain and cut into ¼-inch slices. Marinate in dressing for several hours.

Combine all dressing ingredients, whisking in oil gradually until thoroughly blended.

Arrange lettuce leaves on a platter or individual salad plates. Remove celery root from marinade and arrange over lettuce leaves in alternating slices with tomatoes. Spoon some of the dressing over salad, sprinkle with chopped chives and chopped egg, and serve with any remaining dressing on the side.

Serves 4

CHARD

BOW TIE NOODLES WITH SAUTÉED CHARD AND TOASTED ALMONDS

This dish tastes like freshly sauced ravioli without all the work. The chard, nuts, herbs, and cheese all go beautifully with bow ties.

3 quarts fresh chard leaves (about 2 large
   bunches)
2 tablespoons olive oil
2 tablespoons butter
1 medium onion, chopped
3 cloves garlic, minced
1 tablespoon tomato paste or
   2 tablespoons finely chopped sun-dried
   tomatoes
1 tablespoon fresh lime or lemon juice
¼ cup chicken broth
10 ounces bow tie noodles
¾ cup freshly grated Parmesan or Asiago
   cheese
2 tablespoons chopped parsley
2 teaspoons finely chopped fresh
   marjoram
1 teaspoon fresh thyme
1 tablespoon minced chives
salt and freshly ground pepper to taste
½ cup chopped toasted almonds

❋ Cut out center ribs and stems of chard, and cut these ribs and stems into thin slices. Slice chard leaves into ½-inch strips.

In a large skillet heat oil and butter and add onion and garlic. Sauté until fragrant, about 2 to 3 minutes. Add chard stems and sauté until softened. Add chard leaves and sauté, stirring, for 4 to 5 minutes until wilted. Stir in tomato paste or sundried tomatoes, lime or lemon juice, and chicken broth. Heat thoroughly.

In a large pot, bring 3 to 4 quarts of lightly salted water to a boil. Add bow ties and cook until done al dente. Drain noodles, combine with chard mixture, Parmesan or Asiago cheese, and herbs. Heat through; add salt and pepper to taste. Transfer to a serving dish and sprinkle with the nuts. Add a little additional cheese, if desired.

Serves 4 to 6

FARMER'S MARKET SWISS CHARD

1 red onion, thinly sliced
¼ teaspoon salt
¼ teaspoon sugar
1 tablespoon rice vinegar
1 tablespoon water
1 bunch (about 6 to 8 leaves) chard,
  stems removed, coarsely chopped
3 tablespoons olive oil
grated rind of ½ lemon
2 to 3 tablespoons lemon juice
2 cloves garlic, minced
½ cup chopped Italian parsley
1 teaspoon chopped fresh oregano
salt and freshly ground pepper to taste

GARNISH:
grated Asiago or Parmesan cheese

❧ In a small bowl, combine onion with salt, sugar, vinegar, and water. Set aside for 30 minutes, stirring once or twice. Drain.

Place chard in a large skillet or saucepan with ¾ cup of water and heat to boiling. Reduce heat and cook covered over medium heat until the chard is tender-crisp, about 8 minutes. Drain off any remaining liquid. Add onions and all remaining ingredients and toss with chard. Continue cooking 3 to 4 minutes, or until liquid is gone. Add salt and pepper to taste. Garnish with cheese. Serve warm or at room temperature.

Serves 4

CHARD IN DIJON MUSTARD SAUCE

Another great tasting way to enjoy fresh-picked chard as a featured part of any meal.

2 ½ tablespoons vegetable or olive oil
2 small bunches of scallions, chopped
2 small cloves of garlic, finely chopped
½ lb mushrooms, sliced
1 pound fresh chard, finely shredded
1 tablespoon Dijon mustard

❧ Heat oil in a large skillet or wok. Sauté the scallions and garlic for 2 minutes until softened and tender. Add mushrooms and cook 4 to 5 minutes more. Add chard, cover, and cook over low heat for about 5 minutes, or until chard is tender but still crisp. Mix in mustard and heat 1 to 2 minutes more. Stir and serve immediately.

Serves 4 to 6

GREEK-STYLE STUFFED CHARD

These vegetable, rice, and nut stuffed chard bundles are as beautiful to look at as they are totally delicious to eat. Plan on everyone having second helpings.

FILLING:
3 tablespoons olive oil
2 cloves garlic, minced
2 medium onions, chopped
1 stalk celery, finely chopped
1 cup uncooked rice
½ teaspoon salt
¼ teaspoon fresh ground pepper
2 tablespoons chopped fresh dill leaf
⅓ cup chopped parsley
⅓ cup toasted chopped almonds, walnuts
   or pinenuts
¼ cup lemon juice
1 ½ cups water
¼ cup feta or Parmesan cheese

16 to 18 large chard leaves, with stems
   removed and reserved
2 carrots sliced into ¼-inch rounds
1 cup chicken stock
¼ cup lemon juice
1 cup tomato juice
2 tablespoons good fruity olive oil

TOPPINGS:
Combine ½ cup fresh plain yogurt and
   ½ cup low-fat sour cream
2 chopped fresh tomato

✣ Filling: Heat olive oil in a medium skillet. Add garlic, onions, and celery and sauté until softened. Stir in rice and cook slowly over low heat for 5 minutes, stirring frequently. Add salt, pepper, dill, parsley, nuts, ¼ cup lemon juice, and water, mixing until combined. Cover and simmer for about 10 minutes until all the liquid is absorbed. Set this filling aside. When slightly cool, mix in cheese.

Immerse the chard leaves, 4 or 5 at a time, in a pot of boiling water for 2 minutes or until limp. Remove with a slotted spoon and drain well. Repeat with all the leaves and drain. Lay chard leaves out flat. Mound 3 tablespoons of the filling on the center of each leaf. Fold sides of leaf over center, then fold top and bottom down. Roll each leaf into a compact bundle. (Can be made ahead up to this point.)

Finely chop reserved chard stems and arrange them over the bottom of a large skillet. Lay chard bundles on top, seam-side down. Top each with a carrot slice. Combine chicken stock with remaining ¼ cup lemon juice and tomato juice and pour over chard. Sprinkle 2 tablespoons olive oil over the top. Bring to a boil, then cover and simmer 15 minutes.

Serve with separate bowls of yogurt/sour cream mixture and chopped tomatoes to pass for topping.

Serves 6 to 8

Basque Chard, Lamb, Bean Stew

A wonderfully hearty, but not too rich dish that shows off the traditional ingredient combinations of Basque cooking.

1 ½ cups white beans (soaked overnight in water to cover by 3 inches)
3 tablespoons olive oil
2 pounds lean boneless lamb, cut into 1 ½-inch cubes and 1 lamb shank or lamb bones rolled in 2 or 3 tablespoons seasoned flour
4 large cloves garlic, minced
2 large onions, finely chopped
6 carrots, sliced ½ inch thick
2 stalks celery, chopped
4 cups chicken stock
1 bay leaf
¼ cup chopped fresh parsley
1 ½ tablespoons chopped fresh thyme
2 teaspoons chopped fresh oregano
1 teaspoon chopped fresh sage
1 large bunch chard (about 1 pound) cut into ½-inch strips, stems chopped fine
Salt and freshly ground pepper

GARNISH:
Grated Parmesan or Asiago cheese, olive oil to drizzle

✢ In a large Dutch oven or stock pot, heat 1 tablespoon olive oil until very hot, add lamb cubes and shank or bones and brown on all sides and remove. Add the rest of the oil and heat, then add garlic and onions and sauté over low heat, stirring occasionally, for 8 to 10 minutes. Add carrots, celery, drained beans, chicken stock, bay leaf, and reserved lamb. Bring to a boil, then reduce heat and simmer covered for about 1 hour or until beans and lamb are almost tender. Remove bay leaf and any large bones; skim off excess fat. Add parsley, thyme, oregano, and sage. Mix in chard and cook for an additional 15 minutes. Taste again for seasoning, adding salt and pepper to taste. Serve in soup bowls and garnish with Parmesan cheese and a drizzle of olive oil.

Serves 6 to 8

ORZO, CHARD AND SQUASH CASSEROLE

Mild Muenster cheese tastefully binds this succulent summer vegetable and pasta dish.

1 ½ cups orzo (rice shaped pasta)
1 tablespoon butter
¼ cup chopped fresh green basil
½ cup grated Muenster cheese
freshly ground pepper to taste
1 tablespoon olive oil
2 medium zucchini, quartered lengthwise,
  cut into ¼-inch slices
2 ½ cups sliced mushrooms
10 large leaves steamed chard, coarsely
  chopped, drained
2 cloves garlic, minced
1 tablespoon drained capers
salt to taste
Freshly grated Parmesan cheese

❈ Bring a large pot of lightly salted water to a boil. Add orzo and reduce heat, cooking until orzo is tender, about 10 to 12 minutes. Drain, add butter, basil, cheese, and a lots of freshly ground pepper. Set aside. In a large skillet heat oil, add zucchini and mushrooms and sauté until almost tender stirring frequently, 3 to 5 minutes. Add chopped chard and garlic; continue cooking stirring frequently until zucchini is soft. Stir in capers. Toss vegetables with orzo and add salt to taste. Sprinkle Parmesan cheese over the top.

Serves 6 to 8

CHILE PEPPERS

TO ROAST CHILES

Lay whole chiles directly on a barbecue grill, under a broiler, on a stovetop grill, or over a gas flame. Grill or broil, turning frequently, until the chile skins are evenly blackened and charred all over, but flesh is still crisp. Put the chiles into a paper bag for a few minutes to cool and steam—this helps further loosen the skins. Then peel off charred skins. Rinsing under running water will help remove stubborn bits. Slit and remove veins and seeds. If doing this with very hot chiles, be sure to wear rubber gloves and don't touch your eyes.

Use the prepared chiles in sauces and salsas, in rice casseroles, in omelets, on hamburgers, and in all Mexican dishes. Also great with summer squash, green beans, corn, or homemade fajitas.

GREEN CHILE PEPPER PESTO

An unusual new dip for chips that keeps 'em coming back for more.

6 anaheim chile peppers, roasted, peeled,
   and seeded
1 jalapeño chile, stemmed and seeded
2 cloves garlic, halved
3 tablespoons chopped parsley
3 tablespoons chopped cilantro leaves
½ cup toasted pine nuts or almonds
1 cup freshly grated Parmesan or Asiago
   cheese
1 ½ teaspoons fresh lemon juice
2 to 3 tablespoons olive oil
salt and pepper to taste

❀ Combine all the ingredients in a food processor or blender, adding enough olive oil to make a thick smooth paste. Add salt and pepper to taste. Serve with tortilla chips or raw vegetables.

Serves 6 to 8

DEAN'S PICKLED JALAPEÑOS

When we were the lucky recipients of one of customer Dean's handsome and tasty jars, we knew at last we'd found a master of the pickle art.

20 fresh jalapeño chiles
1 large clove garlic, peeled
1 bay leaf
2 or 3 sprigs fresh basil or oregano
   (opal basil is prettiest)
1 ¾ to 3 cups distilled vinegar

❀ Wash chiles and cut off stems leaving the cap at the top intact. Pierce each chile with a paring knife to allow vinegar to enter the chile. Place garlic and bay leaf in a hot sterilized quart canning jar, then pack chiles tip down into jar as tightly and uniformly as possible. Add basil or oregano sprigs when jar is half full. Bring vinegar just to a boil and pour over chiles. Let sit 2 minutes then tap jar to release air bubbles and top off jar with vinegar to within ½ inch of the top. Wipe rim, seal, and immerse jar 15 minutes in a boiling water bath. Let rest for a few days to blend flavors before opening jars and serving. Refrigerate after opening.

Makes 1 quart

SHRIMP SÃO PAULO

MARINADE:
2 tablespoons olive oil
zest of 2 limes (reserve)
½ cup fresh lime juice
½ cup dry white wine
2 large cloves finely chopped garlic
3 jalapeño peppers, seeds and veins
  removed
½ teaspoon salt
½ cup chopped cilantro leaves

1 ¼ pounds medium to large raw shrimp,
  peeled and deveined
2 tablespoons olive oil
¼ cup chopped scallions
2 large tomatoes, seeded, diced and
  drained

GARNISH:
fresh cilantro leaves

❧ Combine all the marinade ingredients except zest, in a bowl. Add shrimp and marinate for just 30 minutes. In a skillet, heat the additional 2 tablespoons of olive oil, add scallions and sauté until softened. Add drained shrimp (reserving marinade) and sauté quickly for 2 to 3 minutes until shrimp become firm and turn pink. Add tomatoes and reserved zest and heat through. Set aside on a warm platter. Add reserved marinade to skillet. Cook over high heat for 3 to 5 minutes until marinade is reduced by half. Pour over shrimp on platter. Garnish with cilantro leaves. Serve over rice.

Serves 4

Pizza Santa Fe Style

All the Southwestern flavors in a beautiful quick-to-fix summer pizza treat.

one 12-inch commercial pizza crust, ready
  to bake

SAUCE:
1 ½ cups lightly packed cilantro leaves
½ cup lightly packed parsley leaves
2 cloves garlic
1 jalapeño chile, halved, seeded
1 scallion, cut in pieces
1 tablespoon lemon juice
½ cup olive oil
salt and freshly ground pepper to taste

TOPPING:
2 anaheim or other mild green chiles,
  roasted, peeled, seeded, cut into ½-inch
  strips
5 tomatillos (or substitute green
  tomatoes), husked, rinsed, sliced
4 small plum tomatoes, sliced and drained
  on paper towels
1 small red onion, thinly sliced
salt and freshly ground pepper
1 tablespoon chopped fresh oregano or
  ½ teaspoon dried
2 cups grated jack cheese

✤ Combine all sauce ingredients except salt and pepper in a food processor or blender. Purée until smooth. Add salt and pepper to taste.

Preheat oven to 450°F. Place pizza crust on a large baking sheet. Brush the shell with the sauce. Arrange strips of chiles, radiating out from the center. Arrange slices of tomatillos, tomatoes, and red onions in between. Sprinkle with salt and pepper and oregano. Top with grated cheese and bake for 5 to 10 minutes, until edges are crisp, and serve hot.

Serves 2 to 4

Chile Radish Salsa

An authentic and unusual piquant northern Mexican salsa that employs summer vegetables to new and delicious advantage. Delicious with grilled meats or fish.

1 serrano chile pepper, roasted, peeled, seeded, and finely chopped
2 jalapeño chile peppers, roasted, peeled, seeded, and finely chopped
1 anaheim chile pepper, roasted, peeled, seeded, and finely chopped
1 large clove garlic, minced
1 cup finely diced radishes
1 cup seeded, finely diced cucumbers
5 scallions, finely chopped
2 cups finely diced tomatoes, drained
3 tablespoons fresh lime juice
3 tablespoons olive oil
½ cup chopped cilantro
salt to taste

❖ In a bowl combine chiles and vegetables. Stir in lime juice and olive oil. Add cilantro and salt to taste. Refrigerate 1 hour. Drain off excess liquid before serving.

Makes about 3 cups

Carrot-Habanero Salsa

Its bright, hot colors match the taste of this great salsa. Use a whole habanero if you love it fiery hot.

½ Habanero chile, seeded, finely chopped
1 small clove garlic, finely chopped
4 scallions, finely chopped
½ cup finely chopped raw carrot
1 medium to large tomato, seeded, diced, and drained
2 tablespoons chopped fresh cilantro
1 tablespoon lime juice
pinch of salt

❖ Combine and chop together all ingredients: salsa texture should be coarse. If using a processor, process chile and garlic, then add other ingredients and mix together briefly. Do not overprocess.

Makes 1 cup

Gingered Mango Salsa

¼ fresh habanero chile or 1 whole
  jalapeño, seeded and finely chopped
¾ teaspoon soy sauce
1 cup peeled and diced mango
¼ cup brown sugar
¼ teaspoon ground cloves
1 small clove garlic, finely chopped
1 tablespoon finely chopped fresh ginger
pinch salt

❀ Combine and mix prepared ingredients in a small bowl; salsa texture should be coarse.

Makes 1 cup

Salsa Fresca

2 ½ cups diced tomatoes, drained
1 small red onion, coarsely chopped
1 tablespoon olive oil
2 cloves garlic, minced
1 serrano chile, seeded and chopped
2 jalapeño chiles, seeded and chopped
1 anaheim chile, seeded and chopped
½ teaspoon freshly ground cumin seeds
1 teaspoon dried oregano leaves
1 tablespoon red wine vinegar
2 tablespoons chopped fresh basil
¼ cup chopped fresh cilantro
salt to taste

❀ Combine tomatoes and onion in a bowl. In a small skillet heat oil and add garlic, chiles, cumin, and oregano. Sauté, stirring frequently, over moderate heat for 4 to 5 minutes. Combine with tomatoes and the remaining ingredients. Let stand for a few hours to allow the flavors to blend. Drain off excess liquid before serving.

Makes about 3 cups

Spicy Fresh Cilantro Salsa

2 jalapeño chiles, roasted, peeled, and
  stems removed (leave seeds in if you like
  it very hot!)
4 cloves garlic
½ cup coarsely chopped red bell pepper
1 medium red onion, coarsely chopped
1 cup lightly packed cilantro leaves
½ teaspoon cumin seed, toasted, and
  ground
1 tablespoon fresh lime juice
2 tablespoons red wine vinegar
½ teaspoon salt
2 medium tomatoes, quartered, seeded,
  and drained (about 1 cup)

❀ In a food processor or by hand, mince the jalapeños and garlic. Add the remaining ingredients except tomatoes, and process or chop until chunky. Add tomatoes and process or chop until just combined. Set aside for at about an hour to allow flavors to blend. Taste for seasoning. Chill. Drain off excess liquid before serving.

Makes about 2 ½ cups

Garden Hungarian Chicken Paprika

Unbeatable when made with homemade sweet paprika.
A Sunday dinner to look forward to!

3 pounds chicken, cut into pieces
salt and pepper
2 tablespoons butter
2 tablespoons olive oil
1 clove garlic, minced
1 large onion, chopped
3 cups sliced mushrooms
1 ½ tablespoons paprika
1 ½ cups chicken stock
2 anaheim chile peppers, roasted, skinned,
  seeded, and coarsely chopped
2 tablespoons flour
1 cup low fat sour cream

GARNISH:
3 tablespoons fresh chives or parsley,
  chopped

❧ Pat chicken dry. Season with salt and pepper. In a large skillet, heat 1 tablespoon each butter and oil. Add chicken pieces skin-side-down and sauté until golden brown on bottom; turn and brown the other side. Remove chicken from pan and set aside.

Pour off excess fat. Heat skillet, add garlic and onions and sauté until light golden. Push onions to one side of pan, add mushrooms and, if needed, add more butter and oil. Sauté until softened. Sprinkle onions and mushrooms with paprika, stirring until coated. Add chicken stock. Bring to a boil, scraping up bits from the bottom of pan. Return the chicken to skillet along with chile peppers. Cover pan and simmer until chicken is tender, about 25 to 30 minutes, spooning pan juices over chicken occasionally. Remove chicken to a platter and keep warm. Skim off any fat from surface. In a small bowl, whisk and blend the flour into the sour cream, then stir into simmering stock. Simmer 5 to 7 minutes longer, stirring until sauce is thickened. Return the chicken to skillet and simmer for a few more minutes, spooning sauce over the pieces. Serve over noodles. Garnish with chopped chive or parsley.

Serves 4

Corn

Cilantro Corn Pancakes

These Southwestern-style pancakes are colorful and light—a perfect brunch dish. Serve with mild salsa and sour cream to spoon over the pancakes.

½ cup flour
1 teaspoon baking powder
½ teaspoon baking soda
1 teaspoon sugar
¼ teaspoon salt
⅓ cup cornmeal
1 egg or 2 egg whites
1 cup buttermilk or fresh plain yogurt
2 tablespoons vegetable oil
1 cup cooked and drained corn kernels
¼ cup mild chiles, chopped roasted, peeled, and seeded
¼ cup chopped cilantro
⅓ cup chopped scallions
vegetable oil for griddle

✤ In a large bowl, sift together flour, baking powder, baking soda, sugar, and salt. Stir in cornmeal. In another bowl, lightly beat egg or egg whites. Add buttermilk or yogurt, oil, corn, chiles, cilantro, and scallions. Add to dry ingredients and stir until combined. Place a griddle or large skillet over medium-high heat. When hot, brush with oil, then drop batter by large tablespoonfuls onto griddle. Cook until tiny holes form on each pancake. Turn pancakes and brown on other side.

Makes about 12 pancakes

Corn, Tomato, and Summer Squash Soup

A light, easily made soup that is a perfect marriage of summer flavors.

1 tablespoon olive oil
2 cloves garlic, finely chopped
1 large onion, chopped
5 cups chicken broth
4 medium tomatoes, chopped
2 cups fresh corn kernels
1 anaheim chile, roasted, peeled, seeded, and chopped, or 1 tablespoon canned chopped mild chile pepper
4 medium zucchini, sliced
½ cup chopped fresh basil
salt and freshly ground pepper to taste

GARNISHES:
sour cream
chopped cilantro

✤ In a large deep pot, heat oil, add garlic and onion and sauté until softened. Add chicken broth, tomatoes, corn, and chile and simmer for 15 minutes. Add zucchini and basil and simmer for 5 minutes longer. Add salt and pepper to taste. Serve hot, passing sour cream and cilantro for garnish.

Serves 8

Corn and Potato Salad

Colorful and inviting as well as full-flavored, this salad is delicious as a hot dish with fried or baked chicken.

1 pound boiling potatoes
1 cup cooked corn, cut from the cob (one to two ears)
½ cup sour cream or half sour cream and half fresh plain yogurt
2 teaspoons caraway seeds (more if desired)
salt and pepper

❧ Steam or boil potatoes until just tender. Cut into 1-inch pieces. Add corn, sour cream, and caraway and gently toss together. Add salt and pepper to taste before serving as a hot dish.

Serves 4

Fresh Garden Corn Rollups

The fresh flavors of this wonderful vegetable filling are also delicious in pitas, crepes, soft tacos, or to fill burritos.

2 tablespoons olive oil
1 bunch scallions, chopped
2 jalapeño chile peppers, seeded and minced
2 zucchini, diced
2 cups cooked corn, cut from cob (about 2 large ears)
2 medium tomatoes, diced, drained
½ cup chopped fresh cilantro
¼ cup chopped fresh basil
¼ cup chopped parsley
½ cup quartered black olives
1 cup grated jack cheese
6 flour tortillas

❧ In a large skillet heat oil, add scallions, chiles, and zucchini and sauté until softened. Stir in corn, tomatoes, cilantro, basil, parsley, and olives; heat through and add cheese. Add salt and pepper if needed. Spoon a portion of the mixture down the center of each heated tortilla, then top with salsa and sour cream to taste. Fold over ends then roll up into cigar shape.

Serves 6

CORN RISOTTO

Sure to be a favorite, this dish really brings out the nutty sweet quality of fresh corn.

6 medium ears corn
1 tablespoon butter
2 tablespoons olive oil
1 small clove garlic, minced
2 shallots, minced
1 red bell pepper, julienned
1 green bell pepper, julienned
⅔ cup chicken broth
1 tablespoon chopped fresh thyme
3 tablespoons chopped fresh Italian
   parsley
½ cup low fat sour cream or half-and-half
⅓ cup grated Parmesan cheese
salt and freshly ground pepper

GARNISH:
1 teaspoon fresh lemon thyme leaves
2 tablespoons chopped parsley

✢ Cut kernels from corn; set aside. In a large skillet heat butter and oil, add garlic, shallots, and peppers and sauté over medium heat for 3 to 4 minutes. Add corn and sauté, stirring for 2 to 3 more minutes. Add chicken broth, thyme, and parsley and cook covered 8 to 10 minutes, or until most of the liquid is absorbed. If corn isn't tender add a little water and cook for a few more minutes. Add sour cream, cheese, and salt and pepper and cook on very low heat, stirring frequently, until mixture becomes very thick. Spoon into serving bowl and garnish with additional thyme and parsley.

Serves 4

Cresses

Watercress and Fennel Salad with Oranges and Toasted Cashews

Crisp fennel and juicy oranges are complemented by the rich crunch of toasted nuts.

3 fennel bulbs
3 large navel oranges, peeled and sliced crosswise into ¼-inch rounds
6 to 8 large lettuce leaves
½ cup watercress leaves, chopped
⅓ cup toasted cashew nuts

DRESSING:
2 tablespoons balsamic vinegar
¼ cup olive oil
salt and pepper

Cut off feathery fennel tops, chop, and set aside 3 tablespoons for garnish. Trim fennel root ends and cut vertically into thin slices, then into match-sticks. Arrange the oranges and fennel strips decoratively on a platter lined with lettuce. Sprinkle with the reserved chopped fennel leaves, watercress, and toasted cashews.

Combine dressing ingredients, whisking in oil until well blended. Add salt and pepper to taste. Spoon over salad.

Serves 4

CRUNCHY WATERCRESS SALAD

Lots of color, texture, and tast, but no fat!

½ pound mung bean sprouts
 (about 4 cups)
3 bunches watercress
¼ cup chopped red bell pepper
6 to 8 scallions, thinly sliced
2 tablespoons soy sauce
2 tablespoons rice vinegar
4 tablesoopns orange juice
4 to 6 large lettuce leaves

❖ Blanch bean sprouts in boiling water for 5 seconds. Drain and immerse in cold water to stop cooking. Drain thoroughly. In a salad bowl, combine watercress, red pepper, scallions, and bean sprouts. Mix together soy sauce, rice vinegar, and orange juice. Toss vegetables with this dressing and serve on individual salad plates lined with lettuce leaves.

Serves 4 to 6

SWEET AND SOUR WATERCRESS SALAD

2 large bunches of watercress, washed
 and torn, with tough stems removed
6 large lettuce leaves

DRESSING:
2 tablespoons lemon juice
¼ cup tarragon vinegar
¼ cup catsup
1 tablespoon plus 2 teaspoons sugar
½ teaspoon salt
1 teaspoon prepared mustard
1 teaspoon Worcestershire sauce
½ cup vegetable oil

❖ Whisk together all the dressing ingredients and toss a portion of the dressing with watercress leaves. (Reserve extra dressing for other salads.) Line salad plates with the lettuce leaves and mound watercress salad in the center of each leaf to make individual salads.

Serves 6

HAWAIIAN WATERCRESS SALAD

A luxuriant fruited salad in the best multicultural tradition of the islands.

1 head romaine lettuce, separated into
    individual leaves
1 papaya or mango, peeled, seeded, and
    sliced
1 bunch watercress, stems removed
2 oranges, peeled and divided into
    segments or 1 orange and 1 papaya.
    divided into segments or cut into wedges

DRESSING:
½ teaspoon curry powder
½ teaspoon Dijon mustard
½ teaspoon grated fresh ginger
2 tablespoons lemon juice
2 tablespoons rice vinegar
1 teaspoon soy sauce
⅓ cup vegetable oil
2 tablespoons finely chopped bottled
    chutney (such as Major Grey Chutney)
salt and freshly ground pepper to taste
2 to 3 tablespoons toasted sunflower seeds.

❉ Arrange lettuce leaves in a spoke fashion on individual plates. Place papaya or mango slices over lettuce. Sprinkle with cress and diced orange segments (or orange and papaya). Combine curry powder, mustard, ginger, lemon juice, vinegar, and soy sauce. Whisk in vegetable oil, mixing until blended. Add chutney, and salt and pepper to taste.

Drizzle a little of the dressing over each portion. Sprinkle with sunflower seeds.

Serves 4 to 6 (makes ⅔ cups)

CUCUMBERS

GINGERED CUCUMBERS

The flavors of spicy ginger and cool cucumber go perfectly together.

1 large cucumber, peeled
3 scallions, thinly sliced (including part
 of green tops)
2 teaspoons grated fresh ginger
1 clove garlic, finely chopped
1 tablespoon rice wine vinegar
1 tablespoon soy sauce
1 teaspoon sesame oil

GARNISH:
fresh mint leaves

✣ Halve the cucumbers lengthwise, scrape out seeds, and cut into ¼-inch slices. Combine with remaining ingredients and toss to combine flavors. Garnish with mint leaves before serving.

Serves 4

BOMBAY CURRIED CUCUMBERS

Try cooking cucumbers East Indian style for a completely new and delightful dish.

2 large cucumbers, peeled
1 tablespoon butter
1 tablespoon olive oil
4 scallions, chopped (including part
 of green tops)
¼ cup chicken broth
2 teaspoons curry powder
1 teaspoon chopped fresh oregano
¼ teaspoon chopped fresh rosemary
salt and freshly ground pepper
¼ cup fresh plain yogurt

✣ Halve cucumbers lengthwise, scrape out seeds, and cut into ¼-inch slices. In a medium skillet, heat butter and oil. Add scallions and cucumbers and sauté for 5 minutes. Add chicken broth, curry powder, oregano, and rosemary; simmer for 1 minute more. Remove from heat. Add salt and pepper to taste. Stir in yogurt, mixing well, until combined.

Serves 4

CUCUMBER RAITA

Our own version of an authentic East Indian cucumber salad.

2 large, long cucumbers, peeled
1 tablespoon salt

DRESSING:
2 tablespoons finely chopped onion
1 mild green chile, seeded and finely
*   chopped*
1 medium tomato, peeled, seeded, cubed
½ teaspoon ground cumin
1 cup fresh plain yogurt
salt and pepper

GARNISH:
2 tablespoons chopped parsley or cilantro

✤ Cut cucumbers into halves lengthwise and scoop out and discard seeds. Cut into ¼-inch slices. Toss them with salt and marinate for 10 minutes. Rinse cucumber slices in cold water to wash off salt, then drain in a strainer, squeezing them to remove excess liquid. Put in a large bowl. Combine rest of ingredients, except salt and pepper, and combine with cucumber. Add salt and pepper to taste. Garnish with your choice of parsley or cilantro.

Serves 4 to 6

OSAKA STYLE GARDEN NOODLE SALAD

A light, cool, and refreshing salad— perfect for appetites jaded by long days of summer heat.

DRESSING:
1 clove garlic, minced
6 tablespoons rice vinegar
¼ cup soy sauce
2 tablespoons sugar
1 teaspoon Dijon mustard
2 teaspoons grated fresh ginger
¼ teaspoon red pepper flakes
¼ cup peanut or vegetable oil
salt and freshly ground pepper to taste

½ pound Japanese (udon) noodles or
*   linguine broken in half*
1 tablespoon sesame oil
1 pound small cooked shrimp
3 cucumbers, seeded and diced
1 bunch scallions, white part only, sliced
*   (reserve tops for garnish)*
1 cup sliced snow pea pods, sliced in thirds
6 leaves red cabbage

GARNISH:
2 tablespoons toasted sesame seeds
sliced scallion tops

✤ Combine all dressing ingredients, whisking in oil gradually until blended. Bring a large pot of lightly salted water to a boil. Add noodles and cook until al dente: tender but still chewy. Rinse under cold water, and drain. Transfer to a bowl and mix with sesame oil, tossing until coated. Set aside. Add shrimp, cucumbers, scallions, and snow peas. Toss with noodles. Mix in dressing. Line a salad bowl with cabbage leaves. Fill with noodle mixture. Sprinkle with sesame seeds and scallion tops and serve.

Serves 6 to 8

Eggplant

Garlicky Tricolor Pepper and Eggplant Appetizer

Succulent chunks of roasted eggplant and colored peppers combine in this Provençal style appetizer that also makes fine sandwiches.

3 tablespoons olive oil
1 head of unpeeled garlic, divided into cloves
3 different colored bell peppers, halved lengthwise, seeds and stems removed
5 to 6 Japanese eggplants, stems removed
¼ cup chopped fresh basil
2 teaspoons chopped fresh oregano
1 tablespoon balsamic vinegar
1 to 2 tablespoons lemon juice
salt and freshly ground pepper to taste

GARNISH:
3 tablespoons chopped chives
1 tablespoon olive oil
1 tablespoon capers, drained and rinsed

✤ Preheat over to 425°F. Oil a 10 x 15-inch baking pan.

In a large bowl, mix 2 tablespoons olive oil with the garlic, peppers, and eggplant. Spread them on baking pan, with peppers cut-side down. Bake 15 to 20 minutes until eggplant is tender and peppers are blistered and lightly browned.

Remove vegetables from pan and cool. Remove skins from pepper and cut into 1-inch squares. Cut eggplant in 1-inch lengths. Peel and chop or mash garlic.

In a serving bowl mix garlic with basil, oregano, vinegar, and 1 table-spoon of lemon juice. Add roasted peppers and eggplant mixing gently to combine. Add salt and pepper to taste and more lemon juice if needed. Sprinkle with chives and 1 more tablespoon of olive oil and capers. Serve with pita bread triangles or crackers.

Makes 4 ½ cups (serves 6 to 8 as an appetizer)

Japanese Eggplant with Miso Sauce

Savory, but slightly sweet and sour, these eggplant slices are great finger food.

8 Japanese eggplants, halved lengthwise
3 tablespoons vegetable oil

MISO SAUCE:
¼ cup white Miso bean paste
1 tablespoon soy sauce
2 tablespoons dry sherry or mikin (sweet rice wine)
1 ½ teaspoons sugar

GARNISH:
2 tablespoons toasted sesame seeds

❖ Preheat broiler. Mix sauce ingredients together well. Toss eggplant with oil to thoroughly coat. Place on foil covered baking pan cut sides up and broil 6 inches from heat for 4 to 6 minutes, until soft and golden brown (watch carefully). Remove from oven and spread miso sauce very thinly over tops of eggplants. Slide under broiler again just until sauce is hot and bubbly. Sprinkle with toasted sesame seeds and serve immediately.

Serves 4

Baked Eggplant Appetizer

1 large eggplant
2 to 3 tablespoons olive oil
1 large onion, peeled and quartered
3 cloves unpeeled garlic
1 red bell pepper, halved and seeded
1 teaspoon chopped oregano
2 teaspoons lemon juice
⅛ teaspoon salt
⅛ teaspoon pepper
4 ounces feta cheese, crumbled
2 tablespoons chopped parsley

❖ Preheat over to 350°F. Halve eggplant lengthwise. Brush all sides with olive oil. Place halves cut side down on a baking sheet. Bake 25 minutes. Brush onion, garlic, and red pepper with oil and arrange alongside eggplant. Bake 25 to 30 minutes longer, or until vegetables are tender.

Cool vegetables enough to handle. Scoop out flesh of eggplant and place in a food processor or wooden bowl. Squeeze garlic pulp from skins and peel red pepper. Add both to eggplant along with onion, oregano, lemon juice, 1 tablespoon olive oil, salt, and pepper. Process or finely chop by hand. Do not purée. Mix in 3 ounces of the cheese. Spoon mixture into a serving bowl. Sprinkle remaining ounce of cheese around the edge of mixture and parsley in the center. Serve with pita bread or crackers.

Serves 6 to 8 as an appetizer

CURRIED EGGPLANT PATÉ

A handsome and savory appetizer dip.

1 large or 2 medium eggplants
 (1 ¾ to 2 pounds), halved lengthwise
2 medium to large onions, peeled and
 halved
3 tablespoons olive oil
2 cloves garlic, minced
2 teaspoons chopped fresh ginger
½ teaspoon cumin
½ teaspoon coriander powder
½ teaspoon dry mustard
¼ teaspoon cayenne pepper
2 tablespoons lemon juice
salt to taste

GARNISHES:
2 medium tomatoes, peeled, seeded, and
 diced
2 tablespoons chopped cilantro
½ cup plain nonfat yogurt

❉ Preheat oven to 400°F. Place eggplant and onion halves cut side down on an oiled baking sheet. Brush vegetables with a little olive oil. Bake until tender, about 35 to 40 minutes. Put roasted eggplant in a colander, then put a plate on top of it and weight the plate with a heavy can to help drain juices. When drained and cool, remove eggplant, scoop out pulp and discard skins. Finely chop the eggplant pulp and the onions in a food processor or by hand.

In a medium skillet, heat 1 tablespoon of oil, add garlic, ginger, cumin, coriander, mustard, and cayenne, and sauté, stirring constantly for 2 minutes. Add 1 more tablespoon of oil to skillet. Mix in eggplant mixture and cook for 5 to 7 minutes longer, stirring to prevent sticking. Remove from heat, add lemon juice and salt to taste. Garnish with tomatoes and cilantro; serve with yogurt, pita bread triangles, or sesame crackers.

Makes 2 to 2¼ cups

EGGPLANT ON THE HALF SHELL

*A delicious appetizer to scoop out of the "shell" with crackers or
very thin slices of crusty French bread.*

1 large eggplant
1 tablespoon olive oil
2 cloves garlic, minced
1 onion, chopped
1 teaspoon lemon juice
⅓ cup bread crumbs
¾ cup grated Fontina or jack cheese
2 teaspoons chopped fresh oregano
2 tablespoons chopped parsley
salt and freshly ground pepper to taste
¼ cup freshly grated Parmesan cheese

✤ Preheat over to 350°F. Cut eggplant in half lengthwise. Place halves cut side down in an oiled baking pan. Bake 25 to 35 minutes until tender. Remove from oven. Cool.

In a skillet heat oil. Add garlic and onion and sauté until softened. Scoop out pulp of eggplant, reserving eggplant shell. Add eggplant pulp to onion. Using the side of a spoon, mash into onion mixture. Sauté 3 more minutes. Remove from heat. Cool, mix in lemon juice, bread crumbs, Fontina or jack cheese, oregano, parsley, and salt and pepper to taste.

Place eggplant half shells on a baking pan. Spoon mixture into each half. Sprinkle with Parmesan cheese. Bake 30 to 35 minutes until bubbly and golden.

Serves 6 as an appetizer

FENNEL

GREEK STYLE FENNEL

Slow cooking brings out the rich vegetable flavors.

3 large, or 4 small fennel bulbs
2 tablespoons olive oil
1 large clove garlic, minced
2 large tomatoes, diced
¼ to ½ teaspoon salt
¼ teaspoon freshly ground pepper
2 teaspoons chopped fresh marjoram

GARNISH:
½ cup feta cheese
reserved chopped fennel tops

❊ Cut off the stalks and feathery leaves of the fennel. Chop and reserve some of leaves for garnish. Cut fennel bulbs vertically into eight sections.

In a skillet, heat olive oil, add garlic and fennel, and sauté for 3 to 4 minutes. Add tomatoes. Cover and simmer until fennel is tender, 10 to 15 minutes. Uncover, add salt, pepper, and marjoram, and cook over low heat until most of the liquid is reduced. Serve sprinkled with the garnish of feta cheese and reserved fennel tops.

Serves 4

FENNEL AND BABY PEA SAUTÉ

The mild sweet anise taste of sautéed fennel and the bright flavor note of tarragon combine beautifully with tender tiny peas in this delicate and fresh tasting dish.

4 or 5 medium fennel bulbs
2 tablespoons olive oil
1 medium onion, chopped
2 tablespoons lemon juice
1 teaspoon chopped fresh tarragon
1 ½ cups baby peas. (If using frozen peas, defrost partially before using.)
salt and freshly ground pepper to taste

GARNISH:
2 tablespoons chopped feathery fennel tops.

❊ Cut off fennel tops, reserving feathery leaves for garnish. Slice fennel bulbs into thin strips.

In a large skillet heat oil and add onion and fennel. Sauté, stirring occasionally, for 5 minutes, until tender-crisp. Add lemon juice, tarragon, and peas and cook 5 minutes more until peas and fennel are just tender. Add salt and pepper to taste. Sprinkle with chopped fennel tops just before serving.

Serves 6

Hungarian Fennel with Mushrooms

The succulence of mushrooms combines beautifully with the rich flavor of sautéed fennel, finished off in a traditional eastern European fashion. Wonderful as a side dish, or serve over rice for a complete meal.

2 tablespoons olive oil
2 cloves garlic, minced
2 shallots, finely chopped
3 fennel bulbs, trimmed and cut into thin slices
½ cup water
2 teaspoons lemon juice
1 tablespoon butter
1 pound mushrooms, stems removed and quartered
¾ cup low fat sour cream
2 tablespoons minced fresh fennel tops
salt and freshly ground pepper to taste

GARNISH:
1 teaspoon sweet fresh paprika
¼ cup chopped parsley

❉ In a large skillet heat oil and add garlic and shallots. Sauté until softened, about 2 to 3 minutes. Add fennel, water, and lemon juice. Cover and simmer for 8 to 10 minutes until fennel is tender-crisp. If any liquid is remaining in skillet, cook uncovered until absorbed. Add butter to skillet, then stir in mushrooms and sauté until they are soft. Add sour cream and fennel tops. Cook until just heated through. Add salt and pepper to taste. Sprinkle paprika and parsley over top before serving.

Serves 4 to 6

FENNEL ANTIPASTO

VINAIGRETTE DRESSING:
1 clove garlic, minced
3 tablespoons red wine vinegar
1 teaspoon Dijon mustard
¼ teaspoon sugar
½ teaspoon each salt and freshly ground
  pepper
2 tablespoons chopped parsley
3 tablespoons chopped chives
6 tablespoons olive oil

3 fennel bulbs
2 red bell peppers, seeded and cut into
  ¼-inch julienne strips
1 green bell pepper, seeded and cut into
  ¼-inch julienne strips
1 red onion, cut vertically into ¼-inch
  slices, then into ½-inch julienne strips
1 cup cooked garbanzo beans, drained
½ cup pitted, halved Niçoise or
  Greek olives
¾ cup crumbled feta cheese
1 or 2 bunches watercress

GARNISH:
2 tablespoons capers, drained
2 ounces Genoa salami, julienned
  (optional)

❖ In a bowl combine all dressing ingredients except oil. Whisk in oil gradually until thoroughly combined.

Trim root, stalk, and feathery leaves of fennel. Chop and reserve 1 or 2 tablespoons of leaves for garnish. Cut fennel bulbs vertically into ¼-inch slices, then into ¼-inch julienne strips.

In a bowl mix fennel, bell peppers, and onion, and pour boiling water over them to cover. Leave in water for 2 minutes, then thoroughly drain and cool. Add garbanzo beans, olives, and feta cheese. Add vinaigrette dressing, tossing to combine. Marinate several hours in the refrigerator.

Ring a salad bowl or individual plates with watercress. Arrange antipasto mixture in the center. Sprinkle with reserved fennel leaves, capers, and salami if desired.

Serves 6

GARLIC

CLASSIC ROASTED GARLIC

Roasting the garlic makes it mild, rich, and nutty tasting—
a very heavenly spread for fresh crusty bread chunks.

4 whole heads garlic
¼ cup olive oil
1 loaf fresh crusty chunks of sourdough
  bread, cut into chunks

GARNISH:
fresh whole basil leaves

❧ Preheat over to 325° F. Slice tips off of each head of garlic. Arrange garlic heads in a shallow baking dish. Drizzle with olive oil. Bake for 35 to 40 minutes or until garlic cloves are soft and tender when squeezed. (Check to see that garlic doesn't burn.) Remove from oven. Arrange baked garlic heads on a serving platter and pour oil from pan over them. Garnish plate with basil leaves. When garlic is cool enough to handle, dip the chunks of bread in the oil, squeeze out the baked pulp from the individual garlic cloves onto the bread chunks,
and eat warm.

Serves 4

GARLIC-ROASTED CHICKEN

The redolent aromas of roasting garlic and rosemary will make everyone's mouth water in anticipation. Garlic lovers will adore this recipe!

3 ½ to 4 pounds whole chicken
1 teaspoon soy sauce
1 ½ tablespoons Dijon mustard
1 ½ tablespoons olive oil
1 ½ teaspoons chopped fresh thyme
2 tablespoons chopped parsley
12 large cloves garlic, thinly sliced
(about ⅓ cup sliced)
4 sprigs fresh Rosemary
salt and freshly ground pepper to taste

❋ Rinse chicken, removing neck and giblets. Pat chicken dry. Combine soy sauce, mustard, oil, thyme, and parsley. Starting at the neck end of the chicken, reach down with your fingers under the skin past the breast, and loosen the skin around and down to the thigh area. Spread half of the mustard mixture between the skin and meat, then cover with garlic slices. (If some of the garlic goes into the cavity, that's fine.) Stuff cavity with sprigs of rosemary. Tuck in wings and tie legs together with a string so chicken will hold its shape. Sprinkle chicken with salt and pepper. Cover chicken with plastic or foil and refrigerate several hours or overnight.

Preheat oven to 450°F. Remove chicken from refrigerator an hour before roasting. Spread remaining mustard mixture over chicken. Place in a foil-lined roasting pan, breast-side up. Bake 55 to 60 minutes or until juices are no longer pink. Remove from oven and let stand 10 minutes before serving.

Serves 4

KALE

SAM'S STIR-FRIED KALE

2 tablespoons peanut oil
1 teaspoon sesame oil
2 teaspoons minced garlic
1 pound kale, stems removed, leaves cut
   into ½-inch shreds
2 cups sliced fresh mushrooms
¼ cup chicken stock
2 ½ tablespoons oyster sauce
½ teaspoon sugar
¼ teaspoon pepper

✿ In a wok or large heavy skillet, heat peanut and sesame oils. Add garlic and stir-fry 30 seconds, until fragrant. Add the kale and mushrooms, tossing frequently over high heat for 3 minutes. Add the chicken stock, oyster sauce, sugar, and pepper. Stir-fry for another 2 minutes until vegetables are tender-crisp and still bright green.

Serves 4

GINGER KALE

Fresh ginger and garlic add a new twist to the full, sweet flavor of fresh fall kale in this fast easy dish.

1 large bunch kale (about 1 pound) stems
   removed, leaves cut into strips
2 tablespoons olive oil
1 tablespoon butter
2 large cloves garlic, minced
1 medium onion, chopped
1 tablespoon minced fresh ginger
juice of 1 lime
freshly ground pepper

✿ Bring a large pot of lightly salted water to a boil. Add kale and boil 2 to 3 minutes, until slightly wilted. Drain in a colander.

In a large skillet or wok, heat oil and butter, add garlic, onion, and ginger, and sauté until onion is softened. Add kale, tossing until combined. Cover and cook over low heat just until kale is just tender.

Sprinkle with lime juice and toss. Grind fresh pepper over kale and serve.

Serves 4 to 6

GINA'S GARDEN KALE DINNER

A lovely combination of rice with kale, fresh herbs, and prosciutto/cheese topping.

2 ½ cups water
1 cup long-grain white rice
2 tablespoons olive oil
2 shallots, finely chopped
4 scallions, thinly sliced
1 teaspoon chopped fresh thyme
2 tablespoons chopped fresh parsley
½ cup (2 ounces) coarsely chopped
* prosciutto*
1 ¾ cups chicken stock
1 teaspoon grated lemon zest
1 large bunch, or about 1 pound kale,
* stems removed, leaves finely shredded*
2 tablespoons lemon juice
salt and freshly ground pepper to taste
¼ cup grated Parmesan or Asiago cheese

❧ Bring lightly salted water to a boil, add rice, cover tightly and simmer over low heat for 20 minutes without removing the lid. Set aside.

In a large skillet, heat oil, add shallots or onion, scallions, thyme, and parsley; sauté until softened. Add prosciutto and cook, stirring, for 1 more minute. Add chicken stock and lemon zest, and boil uncovered until the stock is reduced by half, about 5 minutes. Add kale and lemon juice, stirring until kale wilts. Add salt and pepper to taste. Spoon hot rice onto a serving platter, then pour kale over it. Sprinkle with cheese.

Serves 4 to 6

KOHLRABI

KOHLRABI SAUTÉ

4 medium kohlrabi bulbs
1 tablespoon butter or margarine
1 tablespoon olive oil
1 clove garlic, minced
1 medium onion, chopped
1 tablespoon lemon juice
2 tablespoons chopped parsley
salt and freshly ground pepper to taste
2 tablespoons low fat sour cream

✢ Peel the tough outer skin from the kohlrabi, then coarsely grate bulbs. In a skillet heat butter and olive oil. Add garlic, onion, and kohlrabi and sauté, stirring often, for 5 to 7 minutes, or until kohlrabi is tender-crisp. Stir in lemon juice and parsley, then season with salt and pepper to taste. Stir in sour cream, and serve hot.

Serves 4 to 6

KOHLRABI AND CARROT SLAW

Sweet carrots and apple-crisp kohlrabi go together perfectly in this variation on traditional coleslaw.

DRESSING:
2 tablespoons very finely chopped onion
½ cup low fat sour cream
½ cup mayonnaise
1 tablespoon Dijon mustard
2 tablespoons lemon juice
2 tablespoons chopped fresh dill leaf
2 tablespoons chopped parsley
freshly ground pepper to taste

1 ½ pounds kohlrabi, peeled and shredded
  (about 4 cups)
2 medium carrots, shredded

✢ In a bowl, combine dressing ingredients and mix well. Add kohlrabi and carrots and toss.

Serves 4 to 6

PICKLED KOHLRABI

These crunchy pickles will beckon to you every time you open the refrigerator.

3 kohlrabi, peeled and sliced ¼-inch thick
2 carrots, peeled, cut into sticks and
    parboiled 3 minutes
2 cloves garlic, crushed
1 bay leaf
3 large sprigs fresh dill

PICKLING MIXTURE:
¾ cup white vinegar
1 ¼ cups water
3 tablespoons sugar
1 teaspoon mustard seed
½ teaspoon dill seed
¼ teaspoon red pepper flakes
1 teaspoon salt

✿ Combine kohlrabi and carrots and pack in a 1-quart glass jar along with garlic, bay leaf, and fresh dill. In a saucepan combine pickling mixture ingredients and heat, stirring, until it boils and sugar is dissolved. Pour boiling mixture over kohlrabi and carrots, filling jar completely. Cover jar. When cool, refrigerate for 3 to 4 days before using to let flavors blend.

Makes 1 quart jar

LEEKS

LEEKS WITH SUGAR SNAP PEAS

1 pound sugar snap peas, strings removed
1 tablespoon butter
1 tablespoon olive oil
1 shallot or 2 scallions, chopped
3 leeks, white part only, coarsely chopped
1 tablespoon chopped fresh marjoram
salt and freshly ground pepper to taste

✤ In a large pot of boiling water blanch peas quickly for 2 minutes. Drain, plunge into cold water to stop cooking, then drain and pat dry.

In a large skillet or wok, heat butter and oil, add shallot or scallions and leeks and sauté, stirring frequently, until vegetables are tender—about 6 to 8 minutes. Add blanched peas and marjoram and stir fry until heated through. Add salt and pepper to taste and serve.

Serves 4 to 6

LEEK, CARROT, AND POTATO SOUP WITH LEMON THYME

A rich-tasting but lean soup that is good served either hot or cold.

1 tablespoon butter
2 tablespoons vegetable oil
2 cloves garlic, minced
3 to 4 large leeks, sliced (about 4 cups)
3 large carrots, sliced (about 4 cups)
2 large potatoes, sliced (about 3 cups)
5 cups chicken stock
*2 tablespoons freshly squeezed lemon or
  lime juice*
1 tablespoon chopped fresh lemon thyme
¼ teaspoon salt
freshly ground pepper to taste

GARNISH:
½ cup chopped parsley

✤ In a 4- to 5-quart saucepan, heat butter and oil. Add garlic and leeks and sauté, stirring frequently, for 6 to 8 minutes, or until leeks are lightly colored. Add carrots, potatoes, and chicken stock and bring to a boil. Reduce heat, cover and simmer until carrots and potatoes are very tender, about 45 to 50 minutes. Add lemon or lime juice and lemon thyme. Purée in batches in a food processor or blender. Return soup mixture to saucepan and season with salt and pepper to taste. Set over low heat and simmer until soup is just heated through. Garnish with chopped parsley. Serve hot or chilled.

Serves 6 to 8

MELONS

CANTALOUPE SALSA

A fresh Caribbean-style salsa: the sweet melon beautifully complements the spicy herbs and chiles.

1 jalapeño chile, seeded
1 shallot
1 scallion, sliced in four pieces
½ green bell pepper, cut into pieces
⅓ cup cilantro leaves
1 tablespoon mint leaves
2 tablespoons lime juice
½ cantaloupe, peeled, seeded, and cut into pieces
⅛ teaspoon salt

❋ In a food processor, combine all the ingredients except cantaloupe and salt. Process until finely chopped. Add cantaloupe and process until cantaloupe is coarsely chopped. (Do not purée.) Add salt and more lime juice if needed to taste. Just before serving, drain off excess liquid.

Makes 2¼ cups

MARINATED MELON WITH HONEY GINGER CREAM

1 ripe melon, peeled, cut into chunks or balls (use any sweet melon variety)
2 cups fresh strawberries, hulled and halved
½ cup orange juice
2 tablespoons brown sugar
1 cup low-fat sour cream or very fresh plain yogurt
3 tablespoons honey
3 tablespoons finely chopped crystallized ginger

GARNISH:
fresh mint leaves

❋ Place melon chunks and berries in a large shallow dish. Combine orange juice and brown sugar and pour over the fruit. Marinate the fruit mixture in the refrigerator for 2 hours. Combine sour cream, honey, and ginger in a small bowl and refrigerate for at least 30 minutes. Spoon fruit into individual serving bowls or a large bowl, and top with sour cream mixture. Garnish with fresh mint leaves.

Serves 6

HONEYDEW MELON WITH MINTED MANGO SAUCE

The tropical tastes of mango, mint, and orange enhance the crisp flower flavor of honeydew and fresh berries.

1 honeydew melon
juice of 1 lime
1 tablespoon finely chopped fresh mint
½ cup fresh raspberries, strawberries,
   or blueberries, washed and hulled

SAUCE:
2 ripe mangos
2 tablespoons freshly squeezed lime juice
1 tablespoon freshly squeezed orange juice
1 ½ tablespoons chopped fresh mint
1 to 2 tablespoons orange liqueur
   (optional)

✤ Halve melon and scoop out seeds. Cut melon into 1-inch chunks and sprinkle with lime juice and mint. Refrigerate, covered, 1 to 2 hours. Peel mangos, slice off flesh, and scrape pit to yield as much of the fruit as possible. Place fruit into a blender or food processor with the 2 tablespoons lime juice, orange juice, and mint and the orange liqueur if desired. Purée until thoroughly blended and smooth. Drain liquid from melon and mound melon in a glass serving bowl. Sprinkle berries over top. Pass mango sauce in a separate bowl and spoon over individual servings.

Makes 1½ cups sauce, serves 6

CHILLED CANTALOUPE SOUP

Herb and fruit flavors blend deliciously in this refreshing light first course or hot summer day lunch.

6 to 8 medium tomatoes, peeled
1 large cucumber, peeled, seeded
½ cup coarsely chopped onion
1 cup chicken stock
½ teaspoon salt
pepper to taste
½ teaspoon ginger
1 tablespoon fresh-grated lemon zest
4 teaspoons lemon juice
1 large cantaloupe, cut into 1-inch chunks
2 tablespoons chopped fresh basil

GARNISHES:
sour cream or yogurt
fresh mint

✤ Purée tomatoes in a blender or food processor until smooth. Remove all but one-half cup to a large bowl. Add cucumbers and onion to the half cup of tomatoes left in the blender and purée. Combine blended mixture in a large bowl with tomatoes. Stir in chicken stock, salt, pepper, ginger, lemon zest and juice. Chill several hours. Combine melon chunks with basil and chill. To finish, combine soup and melon chunks.

To serve: Pour the soup into chilled bowls and put a few spoonfuls of melon into each. Garnish with a dollop of sour cream or yogurt and mint leaves.

Alternate serving suggestion: Hollow out cantaloupe halves, leaving a ¼-inch thick wall and fill with the chilled soup.

Serves 6

Onions & Shallots

Sweet Lemon and Onion Relish

Meltingly delicious with baked ham, lamb, or chicken and a special treat to replace or share the spotlight with cranberry sauce for Thanksgiving turkey dinner.

2 tablespoons olive oil
2 medium onions, cut into thin ¼-inch strips
2 medium lemons
2 tablespoons lemon juice
¼ cup water
5 tablespoons sugar
pinch of salt
1 tablespoon chopped fresh thyme leaves

❖ Heat oil in a medium skillet, add onions. Cover and cook on very low heat, stirring occasionally, until soft but not brown, for about 15 minutes. While onions are cooking prepare lemons: Squeeze the juice from the lemons and reserve. Scrape out membranes and cut the rinds into ¼-inch strips. Put in a small pan and cover with cold water; bring to a boil, then pour out the water. Repeat twice, boiling up the rind for a total of 3 times. When the onions are tender, add the drained lemon strips, lemon juice, water, sugar, salt, and thyme. Cook uncovered over low heat, stirring occasionally, for about 20 minutes, until most of the liquid is reduced and onions and lemons are glazed. Put up in a glass jar. Store in refrigerator for up to a month.

Makes 1 ¾ cups

Cipollini Agro Dolce (Sweet and Sour Onions)

A very traditional dish that earns its acclaim. Use as an accompaniment to almost any main dish or as appetizers.

1 ½ pounds Cipollini or medium boiling onions, peeled
1 cup dry white wine
1 cup water
1 tablespoon olive oil
½ teaspoon salt
¼ teaspoon freshly ground pepper
1 small red chile pepper, halved and seeded (optional)
2 tablespoons sugar
2 tablespoons red wine vinegar
1 tablespoon tomato paste

❖ Place onions in a single layer in a large pot. Add equal amounts of wine and water, enough to cover the onions. Add olive oil, salt, ground pepper, and red chile pepper, if using. Bring to a boil, cover, and boil slowly for 10 minutes, stirring occasionally. Remove cover and add sugar, vinegar, and tomato paste, stirring to combine. Boil down liquid, stirring often, to glaze onions with juices, until the sauce has thickened and onions are tender, approximately 25 minutes. Remove chile before serving.

Serves 4 to 6

Roasted Garlic and Onion Soup

A rich-tasting and satisfying savory soup with the wonderful flavors of roasted garlic and caramelized onions.

4 or 5 whole heads garlic (about ½ pound)
3 ½ tablespoons fruity olive oil
1 tablespoon butter or margarine
2 large onions, chopped
⅓ cup flour
½ cup dry sherry
4 cups chicken stock
2 tablespoons lemon juice
1 cup whole milk
salt and freshly ground pepper to taste

GARNISH:
1 tablespoon chopped parsley

✤ Preheat oven to 325°F. Slice off the top ¼ inch of each head of garlic. Remove some of the outer skin, leaving the head intact. Place root side down in a small baking pan or garlic roaster. Drizzle each head with a teaspoon of oil. Bake 50 to 60 minutes or until garlic is very soft and golden. Cool, then squeeze out each clove of garlic and mince or mash.

In a large saucepan heat butter and 2 more tablespoons olive oil. Add garlic and onions and sauté slowly, stirring occasionally, for 8 to 10 minutes; until onions are golden. Add flour and stir for 5 minutes, scraping up bits from bottom of pan. Stir in sherry, mixing until combined. Gradually stir in chicken stock. Add lemon juice and bring to a boil, then reduce heat and simmer covered 15 to 20 minutes. Add milk, salt and pepper to taste. Heat through and serve immediately in bowls garnished with parsley.

Serves 6

Roasted Shallots

*Roasting makes the shallots caramelize
and become tender, sweet, and delicious.
Wonderful with roasted meat or poultry.*

1 ½ pounds large shallots (about 22 to
  24 peeled) with root ends trimmed
½ teaspoon salt
¼ teaspoon freshly ground pepper
2 tablespoons olive oil
3 sprigs fresh rosemary

✢ Preheat over to 350°F. Arrange
shallots in a shallow baking dish.
Sprinkle with salt and pepper and
drizzle with olive oil. Add the rosemary,
cover with foil and roast 30 minutes.
Uncover and roast for 25 to 30 minutes
longer, until the shallots are tender
when pierced with a sharp knife.
Increase oven temperature to 450°F.
Roast the shallots about 10 minutes,
shaking the pan occasionally, until
browned. Serve hot.

Serves 6

Mushroom Shallot Sauce

*Good with any baked or broiled white
fish or serve over baked potatoes, rice,
or pasta.*

2 tablespoons butter
1 clove garlic, finely chopped
3 large shallots, finely chopped
½ pound mushrooms, including stems,
  sliced
⅓ cup Madeira wine
1 tablespoon chopped fresh basil
1 tablespoon chopped fresh parsley
salt and freshly ground pepper to taste

✢ In a heavy skillet, melt butter, add
garlic and shallots and sauté until
fragrant, about 2 to 3 minutes. Add
mushrooms and cook, stirring frequently,
over moderate heat for 5 to 7 minutes,
until mushrooms are soft. Stir in wine
and cook over high heat for 2 to 3 minutes
more. Add basil and parsley, and salt and
pepper to taste, and heat through.

Makes 1⅓ cups

SHALLOT SOUP CHARDONNAY

A rich tasting but lightened version of classic French onion soup. A wonderful light supper when served with a big salad and followed by a special dessert.

1 tablespoon butter
2 tablespoons fruity olive oil
2 ½ cups thinly sliced shallots
2 cups Chardonnay wine
1 heaping tablespoon chopped fresh thyme
4 cups chicken stock
freshly ground pepper to taste
8 thick slices French bread, toasted
2 ounces (½ cup) grated Swiss cheese
¼ cup freshly grated Parmesan or Asiago cheese

❖ Preheat oven to 450°F. In a 4- to 5-quart saucepan, heat butter and oil over low heat, add shallots and sauté very, very slowly until golden. Add wine and thyme and cook over high heat until liquid is reduced by half. Add chicken stock, bring to a boil, then reduce heat, cover, and simmer for 45 minutes. Taste for seasoning, adding pepper to taste and additional thyme if needed.

Pour hot soup into a large oven-proof casserole or soup tureen. Place toasted bread on top of soup. Sprinkle Swiss cheese, then Parmesan cheese over top.

Place soup tureen in oven and bake for 10 minutes, until cheese is melted and golden brown.

Serves 4

PARSLEY

SAVORY SICILIAN SALSA

Serve with meat, vegetables, or as a dip with chips or thin slices of fresh crusty bread.

2 cups firmly packed chopped Italian parsley
2 large cloves garlic, minced
1 jalapeño pepper, seeded and finely chopped
10 pimiento-stuffed green olives, finely chopped
4 scallions, finely chopped
½ green pepper, finely chopped
1 tablespoon lemon juice
1 tablespoon balsamic vinegar
1 teaspoon chopped fresh oregano
1 teaspoon chopped fresh thyme
3 tablespoons olive oil

✣ Chop all ingredients by hand or combine in a food processor and blend together until finely chopped but not puréed.

Makes 1 ¼ cups

PARSLEY PESTO

A new twist on a pesto. Great with chips, or over fresh baked potatoes.

3 cups firmly packed parsley leaves
3 cloves garlic, finely chopped
1 tablespoon capers, drained
3 tablespoons lemon juice
½ cup toasted pine nuts
½ cup freshly grated Parmesan cheese
½ to ¾ cup olive oil
⅛ teaspoon freshly ground pepper

✣ Purée all the ingredients except oil and pepper in a food processor or blender. Slowly add enough olive oil to make a thick paste. Add pepper to taste.

Makes 1 ½ cups

APPLE-PARSLEY CHUTNEY

*The flavors of the Italian parsley and apples balance beautifully
with the tang of citrus and chile in this lively chutney.*

2 bunches loosely packed Italian parsley
1 ½ jalapeño chiles, seeded and quartered
2 medium apples, cored and cut into
   chunks
grated zest of 1 lemon
grated zest of 1 medium orange
2 tablespoons fresh lemon juice
½ small red bell pepper, seeded and
   chopped
1 ½ tablespoons sugar
pinch salt
2 tablespoons vegetable oil

✤ Trim off and discard parsley stems.
Set aside 4 cups loosely packed leaves.
Place chiles in a food processor and
process until minced (or use a chopping
knife and board). Add parsley and all
the remaining ingredients and process
or chop together until well combined
and mixture is coarsely chopped. Be
careful not to overblend.

Makes 2 ½ to 3 cups

78

PEAS

FRESH GARDEN PEA PÂTÉ

A lovely bright green combination of peas and chile that makes an unusual and delicious, mellow dip.

2 cups fresh peas
1 jalapeño pepper, roasted, peeled, stem
    and seeds removed
2 or 3 tablespoons lemon or lime juice
4 scallions, finely chopped (reserve 2 of the
    green tops for garnish)
¼ cup finely chopped jicama or water
    chestnuts
¼ cup chopped cilantro
salt

✻ Cook or steam peas just until tender. Drain. In a food processor or by hand combine peas, jalapeño, and 2 tablespoons of the lemon juice until puréed. Remove to a bowl and mix in scallions, jicama or water chestnuts, and cilantro. Add salt to taste and more lemon juice if you like. Serve with tortilla chips or crackers.

Makes 1 ⅓ cups

PEAS WITH PINE NUTS AND PROSCIUTTO

2 cups fresh peas
1 tablespoon olive oil
1 tablespoon butter or margarine
2 tablespoons pine nuts
2 shallots or 1 small onion, chopped
4 scallions, including part of the
    green tops, sliced
⅓ cup chopped prosciutto
1 tablespoon chopped fresh basil
1 teaspoon chopped fresh oregano
1 teaspoon fresh lemon juice
freshly ground pepper to taste
3 tablespoons freshly grated Parmesan
    cheese

✻ Steam or cook peas in a small amount of boiling water until just tender. Drain. In a medium saucepan, heat oil and butter, add pine nuts, shallots or onion, and scallions, and sauté until scallions are softened. Add peas, prosciutto, basil, oregano, and lemon juice, stirring for 2 minutes until heated through. Add fresh ground pepper to taste. Garnish with Parmesan cheese.

Serves 4 to 6

BEEF WITH PEAS IN PEANUT SAUCE

A savory Indonesian main dish.

MARINADE:
1 tablespoon soy sauce
1 tablespoon dry sherry
½ teaspoon sugar
2 teaspoons corn starch
1 teaspoon sesame oil

¾ pound lean beef flank steak or top
  sirloin

PEANUT SAUCE:
¼ cup peanut butter
⅓ cup chicken broth
2 tablespoons dry sherry
2 tablespoons soy sauce
1 teaspoon sugar
½ teaspoon prepared chili paste
  with garlic
2 scallions, cut white part into 1-inch
  pieces; reserve tops for garnish
3 tablespoons chopped cilantro leaves
2 tablespoons vegetable oil
1 clove minced garlic

¾ pound snow peas, ends trimmed,
  or sugar snap peas, strings removed

GARNISH:
chopped scallions

❧ Combine ingredients for marinade and mix well. Slice beef across the grain into thin ⅛- x 1- x 2-inch long slices. Combine marinade mixture with beef strips, mixing well. Set aside 30 minutes. Combine all peanut sauce ingredients in a food processor or blender and purée.

Heat the oil in a wok or large skillet. Add garlic and stir until fragrant. Add beef and stir-fry for about 1 minute until meat is browned on the outside but still pink on the inside. Remove from wok. Add more oil to wok if needed, and add snow peas. Stir fry for 1 to 2 minutes. Return beef to pan along with peanut sauce. Stir and toss until sauce comes to a boil and mixture is hot. Sprinkle with scallions and serve right away; serve with steamed rice.

Serves 4

TINY PEAS AND PASTA

4 tablespoons butter
1 large onion, diced
3 cups sliced mushrooms
  (about ½ pound)
2 tablespoons chopped parsley
1 cup orzo (rice-shaped pasta)
2 ½ cups chicken stock
1 cup dry white wine
2 ½ cups tiny young peas
1 tablespoon chopped fresh thyme
salt and freshly ground pepper to taste
3 tablespoons grated Parmesan cheese

❧ In a large heavy skillet melt 2 tablespoons of the butter. Add onion, mushrooms, and parsley and sauté until softened. Remove from pan. Add the other 2 tablespoons of butter to pan and heat until sizzling. Add orzo and stir constantly until golden brown. Return onion-mushroom mixture to pan. Add chicken stock and wine. Bring to a boil, then lower heat and simmer 10 to 15 minutes, or until orzo is tender but still moist.

While orzo is cooking, steam peas just until barely tender. Add thyme and toss with pasta just before serving. Add salt and pepper to taste, sprinkle with Parmesan and serve.

Serves 4

PICKLED SUGAR SNAP PEAS

An unusual pickle that makes great crunchy snacks.

3 pounds sugar snap peas, trimmed and
  strings removed
7 or 8 large cloves garlic, peeled
3 cups distilled white vinegar
5 cups water
2 tablespoons pickling spices
⅓ cup sugar
2 tablespoons coarse kosher salt

❧ Sterilize 7 to 8 pint-sized canning jars. Steam peas for 3 to 4 minutes, then plunge into ice water to stop cooking action. Drain. Drop a clove of garlic into the bottom of each jar. Pack peas into hot jars to within 1 inch of top. In a saucepan mix vinegar, water, pickling spices, sugar, and salt. Heat to a boil, then reduce heat and simmer 5 minutes. Pour hot brine over peas to fully cover them, to within ½ inch of tops of jars. Seal jars and process in a boiling water bath for 12 minutes, then cool. Store in refrigerator for up to 1 month.

Makes 7 to 8 pints

LINGUINE WITH PEAS AND WHITE CLAM SAUCE

2 tablespoons olive oil
1 medium onion, finely chopped
2 cloves garlic, minced
¼ teaspoon crushed red pepper flakes
½ cup dry white wine
two 6 ½-ounce cans chopped clams,
    drained, reserving juice
one 8-ounce bottle clam juice
1 ½ teaspoons chopped fresh oregano
2 tablespoons butter
¼ cup chopped parsley
¾ pound linguine
1 ½ cups small peas
 freshly ground pepper to taste
2 tablespoons chopped chives

❖ In a medium skillet heat olive oil, add onion and garlic and sauté until softened. Add pepper flakes, wine, reserved clam juice, and bottled clam juice. Bring to a boil and boil rapidly until the liquid is reduced by half. Add clams and oregano, stirring over low heat for 2 minutes. Add butter and parsley and reserve while pasta and peas are prepared.

Bring 3 to 4 quarts of lightly salted water to a boil. Add linguine and cook until almost al dente, about 8 minutes. Add peas and cook 3 minutes more, until peas and linguine are tender. Thoroughly drain pasta and peas and combine with clam mixture, adding pepper to taste. Sprinkle with chives. Serve immediately.

Serves 4 to 6

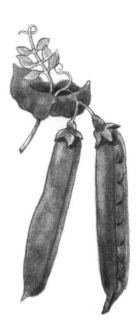

BRAISED PEAS WITH GINGER AND CILANTRO

2 teaspoons vegetable oil
2 teaspoons sesame oil
1 clove garlic, minced
2 teaspoons finely chopped fresh ginger
4 scallions, white part only, finely chopped
    (reserve tops for garnish)
½ cup chopped cilantro leaves
2 cups fresh shelled peas
2 tablespoons water

GARNISH:
chopped scallion tops

❖ In a medium saucepan, heat vegetable and sesame oil. Add garlic, ginger, scallions, and cilantro and stir-fry for 2 minutes. Add peas and 2 tablespoons water. Cover and cook until peas are just tender (don't overcook).

Serve garnished with scallion tops.

Serves 4

PEPPERS

SAUTÉED PEPPERS—ITALIAN CAMPING STYLE

This wonderful simple and totally delicious dish was what every family seemed to cook for lunch when we camped in the Italian lake district a few summers ago. The trick is to sauté the peppers very slowly so you release their natural sugars and essential flavor.

6 large bell peppers (red, yellow, orange, or a combination; never use green, as they aren't sweet enough)
2 tablespoons olive oil
salt and freshly ground pepper

❉ Halve peppers lengthwise, remove seeds and white ribs, then cut them into ½-inch wide strips. Heat enough good quality, fruity olive oil in a large heavy skillet to generously cover the bottom of the pan. Add the pepper strips. Turn the heat down and cook slowly, stirring frequently, until the peppers are softened with just a few browned edges, about 30 to 35 minutes.

Remove the peppers with a slotted spoon onto a platter or into a bowl and sprinkle with salt and freshly ground pepper. Serve at room temperature with fresh cheese, bread, and wine or beer.

Serves 4 to 6

SICILIAN LINGUINE WITH SAUSAGE AND PEPPERS

8 ounces mild Italian sausage, cut into ½-inch slices
3 tablespoons olive oil
2 cloves garlic, chopped
2 medium onions, chopped
2 red bell peppers, seeded and cut into 1-inch strips
1 green bell pepper, seeded and cut into 1-inch strips
2 tablespoons chopped fresh oregano
½ cup chopped fresh parsley
½ cup dry white wine
½ cup chicken broth
12 ounces linguini
4 ounces feta or Gorgonzola cheese, crumbled
freshly ground pepper
3 tablespoons freshly grated Parmesan cheese

❉ In a large skillet, sauté sausages until browned. Remove sausage and drain on paper towels. Discard fat. Heat olive oil in skillet. Add garlic, onions, and peppers and sauté until softened. Remove mixture from skillet, mix in oregano and parsley, and reserve. In the skillet, bring wine and chicken broth to a boil and cook, stirring, until liquid is reduced by half. Add drained sausage slices and pepper-onion mixture to skillet. Cook linguine in boiling salted water until done al dente. Drain. Heat sausage-pepper mixture well. Add hot drained linguine, feta or Gorgonzola cheese, fresh pepper, and grated Parmesan. Mix well and serve.

Serves 6

Lamb Stew with Sweet Peppers

In the best Greek tradition, this full-bodied, flavorful stew brings out the rich taste in its fresh ingredients.

2 pounds boneless lamb,
  cut into 1 ½-inch cubes
salt and freshly ground pepper
5 tablespoons olive oil
4 bell peppers (use a combination of red,
  yellow, and green), seeded and cut into
  chunks
4 cloves garlic, minced
2 large onions, chopped
3 tablespoons chopped fresh basil
1 ½ tablespoons chopped fresh oregano
1 tablespoon chopped fresh thyme
1 bay leaf
3 tablespoons flour
grated zest and juice of 1 orange
1 ⅓ cups chicken stock
1 cup dry white wine

GARNISH:
1 tablespoon chopped parsley

❋ Season lamb with salt and pepper. In a stock pot or Dutch oven, heat 2 tablespoons of olive oil. Add the lamb in batches and brown well on all sides. Remove lamb from pot and set aside. Heat 2 more tablespoons of oil in pot. Add bell peppers and sauté for about 8 minutes, until lightly browned. Remove from pot and set aside. Heat 1 more tablespoon of oil, add garlic, onions, basil, oregano, thyme, and bay leaf. Sauté until onions are softened. Return lamb to pot. Sprinkle with flour and continue cooking for 3 minutes, stirring frequently. Stir in orange zest and juice, chicken stock, and wine. Bring to a boil, then cover and simmer until meat is tender, about 45 minutes. Remove bay leaf. Add bell peppers and heat through. Taste for seasoning, adding salt and pepper if desired. Top with parsley and serve.

Serves 6

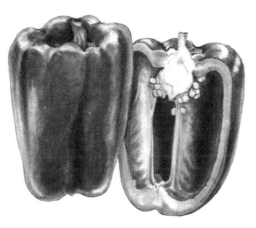

Mediterranean Stuffed Peppers

6 red or yellow bell peppers (or use half
  and half), or green if you are a
  traditionalist
2 cups chicken stock
⅔ cup orzo (rice shaped pasta)
½ pound ground lamb
2 ½ tablespoons olive oil
3 cloves garlic, minced
1 large onion, finely chopped
2 cups sliced mushrooms
2 small zucchini, finely diced
  (about 1 cup)
2 tomatoes diced and drained
½ cup chopped fresh parsley
1 tablespoon chopped fresh oregano
3 tablespoons chopped fresh mint
3 tablespoons chopped fresh basil
2 tablespoons lemon juice
1 cup crumbled feta cheese
½ to 1 teaspoon freshly ground pepper (to
  taste)
1 egg, beaten
¼ cup toasted pine nuts

GARNISH:
fresh lemon or lime slices.

✵ Preheat oven to 350° F. Cut off tops
of bell peppers and remove core and
seeds. Drop peppers in a large pot of
boiling water; boil uncovered for
5 minutes. Remove from water and
turn upside down to drain and cool.
Bring chicken stock to a boil in a large
saucepan. Add orzo, reduce heat and
cook until orzo is just tender, about
10 to 12 minutes. Set aside without
draining. Heat a large skillet and brown
the lamb, sautéing it quickly until it is
no longer pink. Spoon meat into a
colander to drain off excess fat. Wipe
out skillet. Heat oil in skillet and add
garlic, onion, mushrooms, and
zucchini and sauté until vegetables are
softened. Stir in orzo, tomatoes, herbs,
lemon juice, feta cheese, and cooked
lamb. Heat through and add ground
pepper to taste, then stir in egg and
pine nuts, mixing until thoroughly
combined.

Stuff peppers with orzo mixture.
Arrange stuffed peppers side by side in
a greased baking dish. Pour ½ cup
boiling water around them and bake
30 to 35 minutes. Serve on warm plates
with lemon or lime slices to squeeze
over.

Serves 6

POTATOES

ROASTED VEGETABLE CASSEROLE

A hearty meal by itself or as an accompaniment to grilled or roasted meats.

¼ cup olive oil
4 or 5 medium red potatoes, unpeeled, and cut in ½-inch cubes
3 medium zucchini, cut in 1 ½-inch chunks
1 large onion, thinly sliced
4 to 5 medium tomatoes (about 1 pound), diced
½ teaspoon salt
¼ teaspoon freshly ground black pepper
½ cup chopped fresh basil
2 teaspoons chopped fresh thyme or lemon thyme
2 teaspoons chopped fresh oregano
⅔ cup plus 2 tablespoons freshly grated Parmesan or Asiago cheese
⅓ cup water
2 teaspoons white wine vinegar

✤ Preheat oven to 425°F. Oil a 9 x 13-inch baking dish with 1 tablespoon oil.

Combine potatoes, zucchini, onion, and tomatoes in baking dish. Sprinkle with salt and pepper. Add herbs and ⅔ cup cheese, tossing until well-mixed.

Combine water and vinegar. Drizzle over potato mixture. Spread vegetables out evenly in baking pan, then sprinkle with remaining 3 tablespoons of olive oil. Bake on upper rack of oven until potatoes are tender, turning occasionally, for about 50 minutes. Add more salt and pepper to taste. Sprinkle with the remaining 2 tablespoons cheese and bake 10 minutes more. Serve immediately.

Serves 6 to 8

MACEDONIAN NEW POTATO SALAD

1 ½ pounds small red potatoes

VINAIGRETTE DRESSING:
2 tablespoons white wine vinegar
1 teaspoon grated lemon zest
2 tablespoons lemon juice
2 teaspoons Dijon mustard
2 tablespoons chopped fresh basil
½ teaspoon chopped fresh oregano
2 tablespoons chopped parsley
¼ cup olive oil

½ cup thinly sliced scallions
½ cup thinly sliced radishes
½ cup halved Kalamata or Greek olives,
    pits removed
Salt and freshly ground pepper to taste
6 lettuce leaves

GARNISHES:
½ cup crumbled feta cheese
2 ounces chopped dried salami

✤ Steam or cook potatoes until just tender. While potatoes are cooking, prepare dressing: combine all ingredients except oil, then whisk in oil gradually, blending until thoroughly combined. Drain potatoes, cut in half, and toss with dressing. Let cool. Add scallions, radishes, and olives and toss together. Add salt and pepper to taste. Serve on a bed of lettuce leaves and garnish with feta cheese and chopped salami.

Serves 4 to 5

NEW POTATOES WITH LEMON THYME DRESSING

The lemon thyme scented dressing perfectly highlights the nutty sweetness of new potatoes in this delectable dish.

2 pounds small new potatoes, unpeeled

DRESSING:
3 tablespoons white wine vinegar
1 tablespoon lemon juice
2 teaspoons Dijon mustard
1 shallot, minced
6 scallions, white part only, chopped
    (reserve tops for garnish)
2 tablespoons chopped lemon thyme
¼ cup chopped parsley
3 tablespoons vegetable oil
3 tablespoons olive oil
salt and freshly ground pepper to taste

GARNISH:
paprika
sliced scallion tops

✤ Steam or cook potatoes until just tender. Cool slightly, slice into quarters or chunks, and place in a serving bowl. Combine salad dressing ingredients, whisking in oils gradually until thoroughly blended. Pour dressing over warm potatoes, tossing gently until combined. Sprinkle potatoes with paprika and garnish with scallion tops.

Serves 6

ROASTED POTATOES WITH CARAMELIZED GARLIC

These deep rich flavors will warm anyone's heart and palate.

4 tablespoons olive oil
6 to 8 red boiling potatoes, unpeeled, cut into 1-inch chunks
16 to 18 cloves garlic, peeled and sliced (about ⅓ cup)
1 tablespoon sugar
¼ cup balsamic vinegar
2 tablespoons dry white wine
⅓ cup chopped fresh basil
freshly ground pepper
1 tablespoon fresh chopped parsley

❧ Preheat oven to 425°F. Put 2 table-spoons of the olive oil in the bottom of a 9 x 13-inch baking dish and heat in oven for 5 minutes. Add potatoes, tossing to coat them. Roast potatoes, turning occasionally, for 30 to 35 minutes or until tender.

While potatoes are baking, prepare garlic: In a small skillet, heat remaining 2 tablespoons olive oil, add garlic. Cover pan and cook over very low heat for 5 to 8 minutes, or until garlic is tender. Sprinkle with sugar and stir until garlic is golden. Add vinegar, wine, and basil and simmer 2 minutes. Spoon over roasted potatoes. Sprinkle with pepper and parsley and serve.

Serves 4 to 6

TUSCAN POTATO SALAD

Celebrate your homegrown potatoes with this simple, rustic dish that sings with good earthy flavors.

6 medium potatoes, cooked, peeled, and cut into thick slices
2 tablespoons good fruity olive oil
1 large or 2 small cloves of garlic, very finely minced
1 tablespoon balsamic vinegar (don't substitute)
2 tablespoons finely chopped fresh parsley
2 tablespoons finely chopped fresh chives
¼ teaspoon salt
¼ teaspoon freshly ground pepper

❧ Prepare potatoes, set aside. Combine all the remaining ingredients, then toss lightly with potatoes. Allow to stand about ½ hour to blend flavors before serving at room temperature.

Serves 6

BETH'S SUMMER SOLSTICE SKILLET

5 medium potatoes
3 tablespoons olive oil
5 carrots cut into ½-inch or 1-inch cubes
2 cups sliced mushrooms, or whole baby
  mushrooms
½ medium onion, diced
2 cloves garlic, minced
1 pound green beans, cut into
  1-inch lengths
1 tablespoon soy sauce
¼ cup chicken stock
2 tablespoons dry white wine
2 tablespoons chopped chives
2 tablespoons chopped fresh dill
1 ½ teaspoons fresh lemon thyme
1 cup grated Jack cheese
½ cup freshly grated Parmesan or
  Asiago cheese

✢ Parboil, steam, or microwave potatoes until slightly tender, then cut into chunks. In a large deep skillet or saucepan, heat the oil, add potatoes, carrots, mushrooms, onion, and garlic and sauté until slightly browned. Stir in green beans and sauté for 1 minute. Add soy sauce, chicken stock, and wine, tossing until combined. Cover pan and cook over low heat until vegetables are tender. Turn off heat; stir in herbs and mix gently. Sprinkle with the cheeses, then cover pan just until cheese melts.

Serves 6 as a main dish

RADISHES

SMASHED RADISHES

A tangy, appetizing way to enjoy a bumper crop of spring radishes.

1 bunch radishes (about 12 to 14)
1 tablespoon rice vinegar
1 tablespoon soy sauce
1 tablespoon sake or dry sherry
1 teaspoon sugar
½ teaspoon sesame oil

GARNISH:
1 teaspoon toasted sesame seeds
3 to 4 sprigs watercress

✤ Trim off root and stem end of radishes. Lay radishes on their sides and smash with a mallet or the flat side of a large knife. This will create assorted irregular shapes. Place in a bowl and mix with vinegar, soy sauce, sake or sherry, sugar, and sesame oil. Spear radishes with toothpicks and serve in a bowl, garnished with sesame seeds and watercress.

Serves 4 as an appetizer

RADISHES IN CREAM

This appetizing salad is crunchy and creamy all at once.

DRESSING:
¼ cup thinly sliced scallions
¼ cup low fat sour cream
¼ cup fresh plain yogurt
pinch of salt
¼ teaspoon freshly ground pepper
½ teaspoon prepared horseradish
1 tablespoon chopped parsley

1 bunch radishes, thinly sliced
   (about 10 to 12 radishes)

GARNISH:
1 tablespoon minced chives

✤ Thoroughly combine dressing ingredients, add radishes, and mix together well. Serve on lettuce leaves, garnished with chives.

Serves 4

Lemon Honey Radish Salad

2 big bunches red radishes (about 20 to 24
    radishes)
5 scallions
1 teaspoon salt

DRESSING:
¼ cup rice vinegar
1 teaspoon grated lemon zest
1 tablespoon lemon juice
2 tablespoons honey
1 tablespoon grated fresh ginger
1 tablespoon soy sauce

4 large lettuce leaves

GARNISH:
one green apple, thinly sliced
2 tablespoons chopped roasted peanuts

✲ Thinly slice radishes and scallions
and combine with salt. Set aside.
Combine dressing ingredients in a small
saucepan. Bring to a boil, stirring until
just combined. Remove from heat and
cool slightly. Combine sliced radishes
and scallions with dressing. Mound
mixture on 4 lettuce-lined plates.
Garnish with an overlapping ring of
apple slices and top each plate with a
sprinkle of chopped peanuts.

Serves 4

Garden Bulgur Salad

*A new twist on a traditional Middle
Eastern favorite, this minted bulgur salad
features the cool crunch of radishes and
cucumbers and the bright color and
flavor of tomatoes and broccoli.*

3 cups broccoli florets, cut into very small
    (under 1-inch) pieces
1 ½ cups chicken stock
2 cloves garlic, minced
1 cup bulgur
3 tablespoons white wine vinegar
1 teaspoon Dijon mustard
3 tablespoons olive oil
1 cup diced radishes
1 cup diced and seeded cucumbers
½ cup sliced scallions
2 tomatoes, seeded and diced
½ cup chopped parsley
2 tablespoons finely chopped fresh mint
salt and freshly ground pepper to taste

✲ Bring a large pot of lightly salted
water to a boil. Add broccoli and cook
1 to 2 minutes, until just tender-crisp.
Drain in a colander and plunge
immediately into ice water to stop
cooking. Drain again and pat with
paper towel to dry.
   In a medium saucepan combine
chicken stock and garlic. Bring to a boil,
stir in bulgur, cover pan, and remove
from heat. Let stand for about 15
minutes, until liquid is absorbed. Using
a fork, stir and fluff bulgur. Add
vinegar, mustard, and oil. Stir in
radishes, cucumbers, scallions, tomatoes, broccoli, parsley, and mint. Add
salt and pepper to taste and serve
chilled, or at room temperature.

Serves 4 to 6

Spinach

Sesame Spinach

*Subtle oriental seasonings are perfect with fresh spinach
and sesame finishes the dish.*

1 ½ tablespoons soy sauce
1 teaspoon sesame oil
½ teaspoon sugar
2 tablespoons peanut oil
2 cloves garlic, finely chopped
2 teaspoons freshly grated ginger
6 scallions, finely chopped
1 very large bunch fresh spinach, washed
  and drained

GARNISH:
1 tablespoon toasted sesame seeds

✢ Thoroughly mix soy sauce, sesame oil, and sugar. Set aside. Heat peanut oil in a large skillet, and add garlic, ginger, scallions. Sauté over medium heat until softened, 2 to 3 minutes. Add spinach and stir-fry until cooked through but still a bit crispy, about 2 to 3 minutes. Add reserved soy sauce mixture and heat through. Remove from heat, sprinkle with sesame seeds, and serve immediately.

Serves 3 to 4

SPINACH-RICE-PARMESAN PANCAKES

*These pancakes, modeled after some we enjoyed in Milan, are crispy outside
and moist and flavorful inside.*

1 to 1 ½ pounds (1 very large bunch) fresh
  spinach
3 to 4 tablespoons olive oil
1 small onion, finely chopped
1 red bell pepper, finely chopped
2 cups chopped mushrooms
2 teaspoons chopped fresh thyme
1 cup Arborio or other short-grain
  white rice
2 ½ cups chicken stock
⅓ cup freshly grated Parmesan or Asiago
  cheese
1 egg and 1 egg white, lightly beaten
  together
¼ teaspoon freshly ground pepper

❋ Wash spinach thoroughly. Drain, but do not dry leaves. Cook until wilted in just the amount of water that clings to the leaves. Cool, drain, squeeze out moisture, then finely chop. (There should be about ¾ cup.) Set aside. In a large skillet with lid, heat 2 tablespoons of the olive oil. Add onion, pepper, mushrooms, and thyme and sauté until vegetables are tender, about 6 to 8 minutes. Add rice, stirring until coated with oil, about 1 minute. Heat chicken stock separately, then stir into rice mixture. Cover skillet and cook over low heat until liquid is absorbed, approximately 15 to 20 minutes. If rice is soupy, cook uncovered for a few minutes. Cool slightly, then add spinach, cheese, egg and egg white, and pepper, mixing well. Refrigerate mixture until chilled. When ready to cook use your hands to form mixture into 2-inch pancakes, about ½-inch thick. Heat skillet and add enough oil to thoroughly coat the bottom of pan. Cook pancakes in batches, about 5 to 7 minutes on each side, until golden brown, using a wide spatula to turn. Keep finished pancakes warm in a 300°F oven between batches.

Makes 12 pancakes

ASIAN STYLE SPINACH SALAD

*1 pound fresh spinach (1 large bunch),
    washed and stems trimmed*

DRESSING:
1 clove garlic, minced
1 tablespoon minced fresh ginger
¼ cup chopped scallions
¼ cup chopped cilantro
2 tablespoons rice vinegar
2 tablespoons lime juice
2 tablespoons light soy sauce
1 teaspoon sugar
⅛ teaspoon red chile flakes
1 teaspoon sesame oil
¼ cup peanut oil

GARNISH:
mint leaves
⅓ cup chopped peanuts

❧ Place spinach leaves in a large salad bowl. Thoroughly combine all dressing ingredients in a food processor or blender. Add oil in a steady stream, processing until well blended. Toss dressing with spinach, garnish with mint leaves and peanuts and serve.

Serves 4

SUMMER SQUASH

PASTA WITH SHRIMP, ZUCCHINI AND SUN DRIED TOMATOES

Colorful, quick and festive, this zesty dish's aroma will make everyone's mouth water.

1 pound raw shrimp, shelled and deveined
¼ teaspoon red pepper flakes
1 tablespoon finely chopped fresh chives
1 ½ tablespoons fresh lemon juice
salt and freshly ground pepper to taste
1 ½ tablespoons olive oil
2 cloves garlic, minced
½ small onion, chopped
2 medium zucchini, cut into
    julienned strips
1 medium yellow summer squash,
    cut into julienned strips
2 tablespoons sun-dried tomatoes,
    finely chopped
½ pound fettuccine noodles
¼ cup prepared pesto

GARNISH:
chopped basil
freshly grated Parmesan cheese

✣ Toss shrimp with red pepper flakes, chives, lemon juice, and salt and pepper to taste. Set aside.

In a large skillet, heat olive oil, add garlic and onion, and saute until onion is translucent, about 3 to 5 minutes. Add zucchini, yellow squashes, and dried tomatoes and stir-fry for 2 minutes. Add shrimp mixture and quickly stir-fry just until shrimp are no longer pink. Keep warm. Bring a large pot of lightly salted water to boil for the pasta and cook pasta according to package directions. Drain. Return to pot and toss with pesto sauce. Serve plates of pasta with shrimp and zucchini mixture on top. Sprinkle generously with chopped basil and Parmesan cheese.

Serves 4

ZUCCHINI HUMMUS

A new twist on a classic Middle Eastern dish.

1 to 2 tablespoons olive oil
3 cloves garlic, chopped
3 small zucchini, coarsely chopped
1 cup canned or cooked garbanzo beans,
    drained
¼ cup tahini (sesame seed paste)
4 scallions, chopped
3 tablespoons chopped parsley
2 tablespoons chopped fresh basil
¼ cup lemon juice
⅛ teaspoon cayenne pepper
½ teaspoon sesame oil
salt and freshly ground pepper to taste

GARNISH:
chopped parsley
lemon slices

✤ In a medium skillet, heat 1 tablespoon oil, add garlic and zucchini and
sauté, stirring frequently, over low heat
for about 8 to 10 minutes, or until
zucchini is soft. Add more oil if needed.
Place mixture in a food processor or
food mill, add garbanzo beans, tahini,
scallions, parsley, basil, lemon juice,
and cayenne. Process until smooth. Mix
in sesame oil and add salt and pepper to
taste. Garnish with parsley and lemon
slices. Serve with crackers or pita bread
triangles.

Makes 2 ¼ cups

CREAMY GRATED ZUCCHINI

2 tablespoons butter or margarine
2 cloves garlic, minced
6 medium zucchini, grated
1 tablespoon chopped lemon thyme leaves
3 tablespoons low fat sour cream
salt and freshly ground pepper to taste

✤ In a medium skillet, melt butter. Add
garlic and sauté until fragrant. Add
zucchini and lemon thyme and cook
over low heat, stirring frequently, until
the zucchini is tender. Remove from
heat. Stir in sour cream. Add salt and
pepper to taste.

Serves 4

CRUNCHY HERBED ZUCCHINI SLICES

Simple Italian summer fare that showcases fresh zucchini.

6 medium zucchini, cut on the diagonal
  into ¼-inch thick slices
1 teaspoon grated lemon zest
juice of ½ lemon

CRUMB MIXTURE:
1 cup fresh bread crumbs
¼ cup freshly grated Parmesan cheese
2 tablespoons chopped fresh basil
2 tablespoons finely chopped fresh parsley
1 teaspoon chopped fresh thyme

4 tablespoons olive oil
1 clove garlic, minced
¼ teaspoon salt

✻ Toss zucchini with lemon zest and lemon juice. Set aside. Combine crumb mixture ingredients and set aside. In a large skillet, heat 2 tablespoons of the olive oil, add garlic, and sauté until fragrant. Add zucchini and sauté until just tender, about 5 to 8 minutes. Arrange zucchini on a baking sheet with slices touching each other. Sprinkle salt over zucchini and top with prepared crumb mixture. Drizzle with the remaining 2 tablespoons of olive oil. Preheat broiler. Place zucchini slices under the broiler until just lightly browned. Watch carefully to avoid burning.

Serves 4

BAKED ZUCCHINI WITH LEMON THYME

A simple and scrumptious dish that bakes up easily in the oven.

4 medium zucchini (1 pound)
1 ½ tablespoons olive oil
salt and freshly ground pepper to taste
2 teaspoons chopped fresh lemon thyme*
2 teaspoons chopped fresh oregano
¼ cup freshly grated Parmesan cheese

✻ Preheat oven to 350°F. Split zucchini in half and arrange cut side up, on a large sheet of heavy duty aluminum foil. Sprinkle with oil, salt and pepper, herbs, and cheese. Fold up all four sides of the foil into a packet and crimp edges. Bake for 35 minutes or until zucchini is tender.

  * Or substitute regular thyme plus 1 to 2 teaspoons fresh lemon juice.

Serves 4

CHEESE-STUFFED ZUCCHINI BLOSSOMS WITH FRESH TOMATO SAUCE

16 to 18 squash summer blossoms, stamens removed

FILLING:
½ cup grated Jack cheese
1 cup ricotta cheese
1 jalapeño pepper, seeded and finely chopped
½ cup chopped prosciutto or ham
1 teaspoon ground cumin
1 teaspoon chopped fresh oregano
2 tablespoons chopped parsley
1 medium tomato, peeled, seeded, diced, and drained
salt and freshly ground pepper to taste
2 tablespoons olive oil

TOMATO SAUCE:
2 tablespoons olive oil
1 medium onion, chopped
4 large tomatoes, seeded and chopped
1 cup dry white wine
1 tablespoon tomato paste

❊ Preheat oven to 325°F. Mix filling ingredients except oil, adding salt and pepper to taste. Stuff squash blossoms carefully with about 1 tablespoon of filling each; don't overfill. Place in a well-oiled shallow casserole. Drizzle olive oil over blossoms. Cover dish with foil and bake 15 minutes. Uncover and bake 15 minutes longer. While squash blossoms are baking, prepare sauce. In a skillet heat olive oil, add onion and sauté until softened. Add tomatoes, wine, and tomato paste. Let mixture cook uncovered until reduced and slightly thickened, about 5 to 8 minutes, stirring occasionally. Add salt and pepper to taste. Spoon sauce over squash blossoms and serve hot or at room temperature.

Serves 4 to 6 as a main dish

Squash Blossoms Stuffed with Cheese, Spinach and Prosciutto

FILLING:
1 tablespoon olive oil
1 clove garlic, minced
1 medium onion, finely chopped
1 pound fresh spinach, washed, trimmed,
* and finely chopped*
⅔ cup (about 3 ounces) finely chopped
* prosciutto or spicy ham*
1 teaspoon chopped fresh thyme
1 tablespoon lemon juice
¼ teaspoon grated nutmeg
1 teaspoon grated lemon zest
1 cup grated Jack cheese
salt and freshly ground pepper to taste

15 to 18 squash blossoms, stamens
* removed*
3 tablespoons olive oil

✢ Preheat oven to 300°F. In a large skillet, heat 1 tablespoon oil, add garlic and onion and sauté until softened. Add spinach, prosciutto, thyme, lemon juice, and nutmeg and cook, stirring, until spinach is cooked and liquid evaporates. Cool to room temperature. Add cheese and salt and pepper to taste.

Remove the stems and any green ends around the blossoms. Open each blossom on one side. Place a rounded spoonful of filling in each blossom and press edges together. Place them on a greased baking sheet. May be refrigerated a few days if needed, or baked right away.

Brush stuffed blossoms with olive oil and bake for 15 to 20 minutes until heated through. Serve hot or at room temperature.

Makes 15 to 18

BAKED SUMMER SQUASH WITH PESTO CRUMBS

A savory satisfying way to use lots of summer squash. We love it as a whole meal served over wild rice and garnished with toasted pecans.

3 pounds mixed varieties summer squash
3 tablespoons butter
1 tablespoon olive oil
¼ cup half-and-half
¾ teaspoon salt
¼ teaspoon ground black pepper
¼ teaspoon ground white pepper
¼ teaspoon freshly grated nutmeg
¼ teaspoon mace
1 teaspoon sugar
2 teaspoons finely chopped fresh rosemary
¼ cup finely chopped cilantro
2 shallots, minced
4 scallions, finely chopped
½ cup Pesto Bread Crumbs (see recipe 135)

❧ Preheat oven to 400°F. Lightly oil a 2 ½- to 3-quart casserole dish with cover. Trim squash and cut into large chunks (about 1 ½ inches). Arrange squash pieces in casserole and set aside. Melt butter and olive oil together in a small saucepan. Remove from heat and add remaining ingredients, blending thoroughly. Pour sauce mixture over squash, tossing until squash is coated. Cover casserole and bake 40 minutes. Toss squash gently and spoon juices and seasonings from the bottom of dish over squash. Sprinkle with bread crumbs and bake uncovered for 10 minutes longer, until squashes are tender when pierced with a sharp knife.

Serves 8 as a side dish

CAROLINA SUMMER SQUASH SAUTÉ

2 tablespoons olive oil
2 large cloves garlic, minced
4 to 6 baby yellow scallop squash, cut into 1-inch chunks
4 small zucchini, cut into 1-inch slices
2 cups cherry tomatoes, halved
½ cup chopped fresh basil
¼ cup freshly grated Parmesan cheese
salt and freshly ground pepper to taste

❧ In a large skillet heat oil, add garlic and sauté 1 minute. Add squashes and tomatoes and stir-fry 3 to 4 minutes. Add herbs, cover pan, and cook 3 to 4 minutes until squash is just tender-crisp. Sprinkle with cheese. Add salt and pepper to taste and serve hot.

Serves 4 to 6

WINTER SQUASH AND PUMPKINS

BUTTERNUT SQUASH GNOCCHI WITH SAGE BUTTER

A lovely dish that is tender, delicate, and delicious beyond words!

1 large (about 1 ½ pounds) butternut or other full-flavored winter squash, halved, with seeds removed
2 eggs, lightly beaten
½ teaspoon salt
¼ teaspoon nutmeg
2 tablespoons chopped fresh parsley
1 ¾ cups flour
3 tablespoons melted butter
2 tablespoons chopped fresh sage
⅓ cup freshly grated Parmesan or Asiago cheese

✢ Preheat oven to 350°F. Put the squash halves, cut sides down, on a lightly oiled baking sheet. Cover with foil and bake until tender, about 45 minutes. Scoop out pulp and put in a fine sieve over a bowl. Weight down the squash with a plate and a heavy object to press out as much liquid as possible. Let drain for several hours or overnight. Purée the well-drained squash in a food processor or press through the sieve. Measure out one cup. Put the squash purée in a mixing bowl and whisk in the eggs, salt, nutmeg, and parsley, mixing well. Slowly stir in the flour, then beat for 3 to 4 minutes until mixture is elastic and slightly sticky. Bring a large pot of lightly salted water to a boil. Using 2 small spoons, form dough into pieces the size of an almond. Cook in batches of 1 dozen, sliding them into the gently boiling water one at a time. When the gnocchi rise to the surface of the water, let them cook for 2 minutes. Lift them out of the water with a slotted spoon and place on a warm platter. Continue until all the dough is used. Melt butter and stir in sage, then drizzle over gnocchi and sprinkle with cheese. Serve immediately.

Serves 10 to 12 as a side dish

SAUTÉED BUTTERNUT SQUASH WITH SAGE

Slow cooking brings out the butternut's natural sugars, and fresh sage adds a wonderful contrasting flavor accent.

3 tablespoons vegetable oil
1 ½ pounds butternut squash, peeled, seeded, and cut into 1-inch chunks (about 3 ½ cups)
1 large clove garlic, minced
salt and freshly ground pepper to taste
1 tablespoon chopped fresh sage
1 tablespoon chopped fresh Italian parsley

✤ In a heavy (preferably nonstick) skillet, heat oil. Add squash and garlic and toss to coat well with oil. Sauté slowly over very low heat, stirring frequently, for about 30 minutes, until squash is golden and tender. (Add a tablespoon or two of water to pan if squash begins to stick.) Add salt and pepper to taste, then sprinkle sage and parsley over squash and mix to combine well.

Serves 4

BAKED SQUASH WITH ROSEMARY AND HONEY

Rosemary, honey, and butter make the squash both sweet and savory.

2 pounds butternut squash, cleaned and cut into 6 pieces
2 tablespoons softened butter
2 tablespoons honey
1 teaspoon finely chopped fresh rosemary

✤ Preheat oven to 375°F. Place squash skin side up in a greased baking pan and bake 35 minutes, until softened. Turn squash over. Combine butter with honey and rosemary and spread about two teaspoons of the mixture over each squash piece. Bake for 10 to 15 minutes longer, until squash is bubbly.

Serves 6

ROASTED PUMPKIN SOUP

2 pounds pumpkin flesh
1 large onion, unpeeled, halved
3 leeks, white part only
3 cloves garlic, unpeeled
3 tablespoons olive oil
1 tablespoon butter
2 teaspoons minced fresh ginger
1 apple, peeled, cored, and diced
1 teaspoon curry powder
3 cups chicken stock
2 tablespoons lemon or lime juice
1 cup milk
salt and freshly ground pepper to taste

GARNISH:
½ cup chopped chives

❦ Preheat oven to 375°F. Cut pumpkin into quarters or large chunks. Remove seeds and pithy pulp. Place pumpkin and onion halves, cut side down, on an oiled baking sheet along with leeks and garlic. Brush vegetables with 2 tablespoons oil and cover with foil. Bake vegetables for 25 minutes. Remove garlic and reserve. Bake vegetables for 25 to 30 minutes longer until they are tender. Peel vegetables, including garlic, then coarsely chop.

In a 4- to 5-quart saucepan, heat 1 more tablespoon oil with the butter. Add ginger and apple and sauté until softened. Stir in curry powder. Add reserved roasted vegetables and chicken stock. Bring to a boil, cover, and simmer for 15 minutes or until vegetables are very tender. Stir in lemon or lime juice. Purée the mixture in batches in a blender or food processor. Return the soup to pot, add milk, and heat through just until warm. Add salt and pepper to taste. Garnish with chives and serve.

Serves 6

Laura's Glazed Pumpkin Ginger Bars

Pumpkin, spices, and candied ginger perfectly complement each other in these bar cookies that have become a Thanksgiving tradition with us.

1 ¾ cups unbleached flour
1 teaspoon baking powder
½ teaspoon baking soda
½ teaspoon salt
1 teaspoon cinnamon
½ teaspoon ground ginger
½ teaspoon nutmeg
½ teaspoon allspice
½ cup butter, at room temperature
1 cup lightly packed dark brown sugar
1 egg
1 teaspoon vanilla extract
1 cup cooked, puréed pumpkin
½ cup chopped walnuts or pecans
½ cup chopped candied ginger

GLAZE:
1 cup sifted confectioners' sugar
2 teaspoons grated orange zest
3 to 4 tablespoons orange juice

✻ Preheat oven to 350°F. Grease a 10 x 15-inch baking pan. Sift together flour, baking powder, baking soda, salt, cinnamon, ground ginger, nutmeg, and allspice. Set aside.

In a large mixing bowl, beat butter until creamy then add brown sugar, beating until fluffy. Add egg, vanilla, and pumpkin, beating well. Add dry ingredients, mixing until batter is smooth. Stir in nuts and candied ginger. Spoon batter into prepared pan. Bake for 15 to 18 minutes or until cake pulls away from sides of pan.

Combine confectioners' sugar with orange zest. Add orange juice gradually to confectioners' sugar, adding just enough to give the proper consistency for spreading. Spread on the warm bars. When cool, cut into diamonds or squares and store covered for a day to let flavors blend before serving .

Makes 4 dozen

Pumpkin Date Nut Cake

1 pound pumpkin flesh
2 cups unbleached flour
2 teaspoons baking powder
1 ½ teaspoons baking soda
1 ½ teaspoons ground ginger
1 ½ teaspoons ground cinnamon
¼ teaspoon salt
2 eggs
2 egg whites
½ cup granulated sugar
½ cup firmly packed dark brown sugar
1 tablespoon grated orange zest
1 teaspoon vanilla extract
1 cup fresh plain yogurt
2 tablespoons melted butter
1 cup chopped, pitted soft dates, sprinkled
  with 1 tablespoon flour
⅓ cup chopped almonds (optional)

GLAZE:
¾ cup powdered sugar
1 tablespoon orange juice
1 tablespoon orange liqueur (optional)

❖ Preheat oven to 350°F. Steam or bake pumpkin until tender. When cool, mash with a fork and measure out one full cup of pulp. Grease and flour a medium bundt pan. Sift dry ingredients together and set aside.

In a large bowl, beat eggs and egg whites until thick. Add granulated sugar, brown sugar, orange zest, vanilla, and yogurt, blending well. Stir in the mashed pumpkin and melted butter. Add dry ingredients along with dates and nuts, mixing until just combined. Pour into prepared pan and bake 45 to 50 minutes, or until a wooden pick inserted in center comes out clean. Meanwhile, whisk together glaze ingredients. Let cake cool on a rack for 10 minutes, then turn out and brush with glaze. Best if let rest one or two days before serving to let flavors blend.

Serves 8 to 10

TOMATILLOS

TOMATILLO-POBLANO SAUCE FOR FISH OR ENCHILADAS

A perfect piquant flavor enhancer for freshly grilled fish, or as an enchilada sauce.

8 to 10 fresh tomatillos
3 large poblano chile peppers, roasted, peeled and seeded
1 small whole jalapeño chile pepper, roasted
2 cloves garlic, halved
¾ cup chicken stock
½ cup lightly packed fresh cilantro leaves
salt to taste

❧ Peel husks off tomatillos and rinse well. In a medium saucepan cover tomatillos with water. Bring to a boil. Reduce heat and simmer covered for 5 minutes. Drain, leaving tomatillos in saucepan. Add chiles, garlic, and chicken stock. Simmer covered for 10 minutes. Cool. Pour mixture into a blender or food processor with cilantro and purée. Remove to a bowl and add salt to season.

Makes 2 ½ cups

TOMATILLO SALSA

A simple, tasty, fresh salsa for spooning over chicken or fish—or to enjoy as a dip with chips.

12 tomatillos
2 whole jalapeño chiles, stems removed
2 cloves garlic, minced
2 tablespoons chopped cilantro
2 tablespoons lime juice
salt to taste

❧ Place tomatillos and jalapeños in a small saucepan with enough water to cover. Simmer for about 4 to 5 minutes. Drain and place in a food processor or blender with the garlic, cilantro, and lime juice. Process until coarsely chopped. Add salt to taste.

Makes 1 ½ cups

ZUCCHINI TOMATILLO BISQUE

A smooth, slightly piquant, and very satisfying soup.

2 tablespoons vegetable or olive oil
2 tablespoons butter or margarine
2 cloves garlic, finely chopped
2 medium onions, coarsely chopped
6 medium zucchini, chopped or
    coarsely grated
2 anaheim chiles, roasted, peeled, seeded,
    and chopped
1 jalapeño chile, stem removed, seeded,
    and chopped
6 tomatillos, husked and chopped
6 cups chicken stock
5 corn tortillas
1 to 2 tablespoons lime juice
⅓ cup cilantro leaves, chopped
salt and freshly ground pepper to taste

OPTIONAL GARNISHES:
sour cream
crumbled tortilla chips
cilantro leaves

✢ In a large saucepan, heat oil and butter, add garlic and onions and sauté until softened. Add zucchini, chiles, and tomatillos, stirring until coated and heated through. Add chicken stock; bring to a boil, then cover and simmer for about 20 minutes or until zucchini is tender. Tear or shred tortillas into pieces and add to soup mixture. Stir in lime juice and cilantro leaves. In a blender or food processor, blend soup in batches until puréed and smooth. Return to saucepan and heat through. Add salt and pepper to taste. Serve hot accompanied with a dollop of sour cream and a few crumbled tortilla chips and cilantro leaves. This is a very thick soup; if you prefer it thinner, stir in a little more chicken stock before serving.

Makes about 10 cups

TOMATOES

CHERRY TOMATO AND HERB STIR-FRY

Fast cooking perfectly marries the flavors of herbs and sweet, tart tomatoes.

1 pint (about 3 dozen) cherry tomatoes,
*   stemmed, washed, and patted dry*
1 tablespoon butter
1 tablespoon olive oil
1 large clove garlic, minced
1 shallot or 2 scallions, minced
⅓ cup chopped fresh basil
1 tablespoons chopped fresh oregano
salt and freshly ground pepper to taste

❋ In a large skillet, heat butter and oil. Add garlic and shallot or scallions and sauté for 2 to 3 minutes, until fragrant. Add tomatoes and herbs, shaking pan continuously for 2 to 3 minutes, until heated through. Do not overcook. Season with salt and pepper to taste. Serve immediately.

Serves 4

HERBED TOMATO AND CHEESE APPETIZER DIP

A delicious appetizer dip full of summer flavors. Great served with crackers, raw vegetables, and shrimp.

4 medium to large ripe tomatoes
3 large unpeeled garlic cloves
1 ½ teaspoons grated lemon zest
1 teaspoon lemon juice
½ teaspoon sugar
¼ teaspoon Tabasco sauce
¼ teaspoon salt
¼ teaspoon freshly ground pepper
1 tablespoon chopped fresh mint
2 tablespoons chopped fresh basil
¼ cup ricotta cheese

GARNISH:
mixture of 1 tablespoon each
*   chopped mint, basil, and parsley*

❋ Preheat oven to 375°F. Place the tomatoes and garlic in a small baking pan. Roast in the oven for about 20 minutes, until skins of tomatoes split. Peel tomatoes and garlic and crush in a heavy skillet. Add lemon zest, lemon juice, sugar, Tabasco, salt, and pepper. Cover pan and cook over low heat for 20 minutes. Uncover pan and cook over medium heat, stirring frequently, until liquid is absorbed and tomatoes are the consistency of paste. Add mint, basil, parsley and heat through. Let cool slightly, then add ricotta. Refrigerate until ready to serve. Garnish by topping with chopped mixed herbs.

Makes 1 ¼ cups

GREEN AND RED TOMATO SALAD

A great way to end the tomato season!

DRESSING:
1 large clove garlic, finely chopped
½ teaspoon salt
⅛ teaspoon freshly ground pepper
2 tablespoons lemon juice
3 tablespoons wine vinegar
½ cup olive oil
½ teaspoon ground cumin

3 large green tomatoes, picked just before
they begin to ripen to red
3 large red-ripe tomatoes
1 medium red onion
3 tablespoons coarsely chopped fresh basil

✷ Thoroughly combine all dressing ingredients. Set aside. Cube tomatoes. Cut onion into thin slices and separate into rings. Combine tomatoes and onions in a salad bowl with the chopped basil. Add dressing and toss. Let sit about ½ hour to blend flavors. Delicious with barbecue!

Serves 6

TOMATO TART

Ripe red tomatoes baked with a cheesy herbed filling makes a savory, colorful tart. Serve with green salad and fresh French bread to mop up the juices.

1 9-inch pie crust, pre-baked 5 minutes
3 to 4 medium tomatoes, cored, seeded,
and cut into thick slices
salt and freshly ground pepper to taste
1 tablespoon olive oil
1 clove garlic, minced
1 medium onion, finely chopped
¼ cup freshly grated Parmesan cheese
2 eggs
1 cup whole milk
½ cup grated Fontina or Jack cheese
½ cup chopped fresh basil
2 tablespoons chopped fresh parsley
2 tablespoons chopped fresh chives

✷ Preheat oven to 375°F. Put tomato slices on paper towels; pat slices to remove excess moisture. Sprinkle with salt and pepper. In a small skillet, heat oil and sauté garlic and onion until softened. Let cool. Sprinkle 3 tablespoons of Parmesan cheese over crust. Top with sautéed onion mixture and lay tomato slices in a pretty pattern on top.

In a bowl beat eggs well, then add milk, Fontina or Jack cheese, basil, and parsley, mixing until thoroughly combined. Pour mixture over tomatoes in the pie crust. Sprinkle with the remaining tablespoon of Parmesan cheese and the chives. Bake 35-40 minutes or until puffed and golden. Let cool on a rack for a few minutes before cutting.

Serves 6

BENJAMIN'S GREEN TOMATO MINCEMEAT

*Wonderful for pie, tart, or cookie fillings, or served on
crisp whole wheat crackers with cream cheese.*

7 cups finely chopped very green tomatoes
7 cups finely chopped tart, firm green
   apples
1 whole lemon, finely chopped or ground,
   including rind
3 cups raisins
3 cups firmly packed brown sugar
1 cup white sugar
3 tablespoons light molasses
1 ½ cups apple cider vinegar
½ cup brandy
1 tablespoon cinnamon
1 teaspoon ground cloves
¾ teaspoon ground allspice
¾ teaspoon ground nutmeg
1 ½ teaspoons salt
¾ teaspoon ground black pepper
½ cup butter

✻ Mix together all ingredients except butter in a deep, heavy-bottomed kettle. Bring to a boil and immediately turn down heat so mixture will bubble gently. Cook uncovered over medium to low heat, stirring regularly to prevent sticking, for 3 hours or until mixture is thick and liquid is absorbed. (Watch and lower heat if mixture is spattering.) After about an hour and a half, begin to taste often. If liquid seems to be evaporating too quickly, add additional vinegar or brandy, depending on taste. If mixture seems too tart, add more sugar. Once mincemeat is cooked down to desired thickness, mix in butter a little bit at a time until well combined. Can or freeze, or store in the refrigerator for up to a month.

Makes 3 quarts of rich aromatic spicy-brown mincemeat, enough for 6 small pies

Bruschetta with Summer Tomatoes

A traditional grilled Italian treat that tastes heavenly with vine-ripe tomatoes. Serve with chicken, fish, or hamburgers from the barbecue.

2 cloves garlic, finely chopped
3 ripe red tomatoes, seeded, coarsely
  chopped, and drained
¼ cup chopped fresh basil
¼ cup chopped fresh Italian parsley
⅓ cup olive oil
½ teaspoon each salt
½ teaspoon freshly ground pepper
8 thick slices crusty Italian or
  French bread

❧ Combine all ingredients except bread and reserve. Grill bread slices on both sides on the barbecue grill until toasted and marked with grill marks (or toast bread well). Top with tomato mixture and serve immediately.

Serves 4

Plum Tomato Chutney

Serve over grilled chicken, fish, lamb, pork or as a dressing over shredded cabbage.

1 ½ quarts coarsely chopped ripe plum
  tomatoes
6 cloves garlic, minced
1 large onion, finely chopped
½ cup chopped crystallized ginger
1 cup raisins
grated zest and juice of 1 orange
1 ½ cups firmly packed light brown sugar
1 cup white vinegar
2 whole cinnamon sticks
½ teaspoon salt
½ cup slivered almonds (optional)

❧ In a large saucepan, combine all ingredients and bring to boil. Reduce heat, cover and simmer for 1 ½ hours, stirring occasionally. Add almonds. Uncover and cook rapidly until slightly thickened. Ladle into hot sterilized jars; seal and process according to manufacturer's directions. Store in a cool, dry, dark place.

Makes 5 cups

Green Tomato Salsa

An unusual new salsa packed with zesty late summer flavors.

4 or 5 large green tomatoes
1 red bell pepper
1 or 2 serrano chiles, roasted and peeled
    but not seeded
1 small red onion, quartered
2 cloves garlic, minced
½ teaspoon sugar
½ teaspoon cumin
½ cup fresh cilantro leaves
salt to taste

✣ Char tomatoes, bell pepper, and chiles over a direct flame or under a broiler until blackened on all sides, then place in a plastic bag to steam for 10 minutes. Rub off charred skins. Halve and remove ribs and seeds from bell pepper. Core and halve tomatoes and combine with remaining ingredients in a food processor. Process just until coarsely chopped. Add salt to taste and serve with crispy chips.

Makes 3 cups

Chunky Green and Red Tomato Sauce

Another great way to enjoy the last of the season's harvest. Serve over rice, polenta, or pasta.

3 tablespoons olive oil
4 cloves garlic, minced
2 large onions, chopped
1 ½ pounds (about 6) green tomatoes,
    coarsely chopped
1 ½ pounds (about 6) red tomatoes,
    coarsely chopped
1 large carrot, grated
½ cup chicken stock
1 cup tomato purée
⅓ cup dry red wine
¼ cup chopped fresh parsley
1 tablespoon chopped fresh oregano
2 teaspoons chopped fresh thyme
4 sage leaves
1 small dried chile, crumbled
salt and freshly ground pepper to taste

✣ In a heavy bottomed saucepan heat olive oil. Add garlic and onions and sauté very slowly 12 to 15 minutes until onions are softened and light golden in color. Add green and red tomatoes, carrot, chicken stock, tomato purée, wine, herbs, and spices. Stir together, bring to a boil, then cover and simmer for 30 to 40 minutes. Uncover and stir well to blend. Add salt and, if needed, pepper to taste.

Makes 6 cups

TURNIPS

GOLDEN TOPPED CHEESY POTATO, ONION AND TURNIP CASSEROLE

The caramelized onions combine perfectly with the sweetness of potatoes and turnips in this satisfying casserole. Real comfort food!

3 tablespoons butter
1 tablespoon olive oil
2 large onions, thinly sliced
2 large baking potatoes (about 1 pound),
  thinly sliced
2 medium turnips, thinly sliced
salt and freshly ground pepper to taste
1 ½ tablespoons finely chopped fresh
  marjoram
1 ½ cups grated Swiss cheese
2 tablespoons freshly grated Parmesan
  cheese
1 ½ cups milk
¼ cup seasoned bread or cracker crumbs
⅓ cup chopped parsley

✤ Preheat over to 375°F. Thoroughly grease an 8 x 11-inch shallow baking dish. Melt 1 tablespoon of the butter and olive oil together in a large skillet. Sauté onions slowly over low heat until golden brown, about 15 to 18 minutes. In the baking dish, make an even layer using half the potatoes and turnips, seasoning with salt and pepper and a little of the marjoram. Layer with half the onions and half the cheeses. Dot with 1 tablespoon of the butter. Make a second layer with the remaining ingredients in same order. Pour milk over gently and top with bread crumbs and parsley. Bake covered for 45 minutes, then uncover and continue to bake 15 to 20 minutes longer, until vegetables are tender and top is golden. Serve hot.

Serves 6 to 8

KIMCHEE-STYLE TURNIPS

A new treat for kimchee lovers.

4 turnips, sliced ⅛-inch thick
  (about 1 ¼ pounds)
salt

MARINADE:
½ cup water
2 tablespoons rice vinegar
2 tablespoons soy sauce
2 tablespoons sugar
2 small slices fresh ginger
1 clove garlic, minced
3 scallions, cut into 1-inch lengths
¼ teaspoon red chile flakes

GARNISH:
1 tablespoon chopped chives
2 teaspoons toasted sesame seeds

❖ Sprinkle turnip slices with salt. Set aside for 2 hours. Rinse and drain. In a saucepan combine marinade ingredients and bring to a boil. Add turnips and toss with mixture. Cook until liquid comes to a boil. Cool; place turnips and liquid in a jar. Refrigerate. Shake jar occasionally to distribute liquid; allow flavors to blend overnight. Serve garnished with chives and sesame seeds.

Makes 3 to 4 cups

Salads and Salad Dressings

FRAN'S COBB SALAD

*A whole meal salad that is a meal in itself—an elegant luncheon dish or a light,
satisfying supper. Lay out the smorgasbord of ingredients in the
salad bowl in a spiral.*

DRESSING:
1 teaspoon dry mustard
¼ teaspoon sugar
½ teaspoon salt
½ teaspoon freshly ground pepper
1 small clove garlic, finely chopped or
 crushed
¼ cup balsamic or red wine vinegar
1 tablespoon lemon juice
1 teaspoon Worcestershire sauce
⅔ cup olive oil

1 head butter lettuce
6 cups shredded crispy head lettuce
1 whole chicken breast, cooked, skinned,
 boned, and diced
1 bunch watercress, finely chopped
6 slices crisply cooked bacon, crumbled
3 hard-cooked eggs, diced
3 medium tomatoes, peeled, seeded,
 and diced
1 ripe avocado, peeled and diced
½ cup Roquefort or blue cheese, crumbled
2 tablespoons chopped chives

❧ Whisk together dressing ingredients.
Line individual salad plates or a large
platter with butter lettuce leaves. Spread
shredded lettuce over butter lettuce
leaves. Arrange chicken, watercress,
bacon, eggs, tomatoes, and avocado in
rows on top of lettuce. Sprinkle with
cheese and chives. Serve arranged salad
and add dressing at the table.

Serves 6

Tommy's Tampa Caesar Salad

Worth a trip to Tampa, where Tom Shepherd never fails to delight the family with his own "secret" Caesar salad. Here it is at last.

✤ Combine 2 crushed or minced garlic cloves with ½ cup good fruity olive oil. Let blend 6 to 8 hours. Put 2 tablespoons of this garlic oil into a large skillet. Add 1 ½ to 2 cups cubed French bread. Sauté until lightly browned, add salt and pepper to taste. Reserve.

Chop one can of anchovies fine and then mash them up very well into a paste with their own oil. Combine with the rest of the garlic oil. Add ¼ teaspoon dry mustard and a few generous grindings of fresh pepper (to taste). Add 4 drops Worcestershire sauce, 3 tablespoons wine vinegar and the juice of one big fresh lemon.

Tear up 2 heads of fresh Romaine leaves into serving size pieces, then pour the dressing over them. Top with the garlic croutons, sprinkle over ⅓ cup freshly shredded Parmesan cheese. Enjoy immediately.

Serves 6

Arugula with Raspberry Poppyseed Vinaigrette

3 tablespoons raspberry vinegar
1 tablespoon sugar
1 teaspoon Dijon mustard
2 tablespoons chopped red onion
¼ teaspoon salt
½ cup vegetable oil
1 tablespoon poppy seeds
3 cups arugula leaves
2 pears, thinly sliced

GARNISH:
toasted cashews or pecans, chopped

✤ In a blender or food processor, combine vinegar, sugar, mustard, onion, and salt. Process until mixed. In a steady stream, add oil until combined. Stir in poppy seeds. If not using immediately store in refrigerator. Shake very well before using. Serve over arugula and sliced fresh pears. Garnish with toasted chopped nuts.

Serves 4

Orange and Mint Salad

3 oranges
½ clove garlic, halved
¼ teaspoon salt
¼ teaspoon dry mustard
2 tablespoons rice vinegar
¼ cup olive oil
freshly ground pepper to taste
¼ cup chopped fresh mint leaves
1 large head lettuce, torn into bite-size
   pieces

✣ Grate the zest of one of the oranges, then juice the orange to make ¼ cup juice. Peel and section the other 2 oranges and set aside for garnish. In a salad bowl, rub garlic in salt and mustard. Add vinegar. Whisk in olive oil and pepper to taste. Remove garlic. Toss with mint leaves, lettuce, and reserved oranges. Sprinkle with the grated orange zest.

Serves 4

Mesclun Salad with Walnuts and Grapes

The piquant flavors and crunchy texture of mesclun greens tossed with sweet juicy grapes and toasted nuts make an unusual and memorable salad combination.

DRESSING:
3 tablespoons balsamic vinegar
2 teaspoons grated orange zest
3 tablespoons orange juice
1 tablespoon chopped fresh tarragon
3 tablespoons olive oil
3 tablespoons vegetable oil
salt and freshly ground pepper to taste

1 quart mixed mesclun salad greens,
   washed and dried
1 cup red Flame or other seedless red
   grapes
⅓ cup toasted chopped walnuts

✣ In a small bowl combine vinegar, orange zest, juice, and tarragon. Add oils gradually, whisking until thoroughly combined. Place greens in a salad bowl and toss with dressing. Sprinkle grapes and nuts over salad just before serving.

Serves 4 (makes ½ cup dressing)

Hot Wilted Spring Greens

If you use tender young greens of a uniform size, they'll cook in just a minute or two. If plants are older, cut leaves into ribbons crosswise—this tenderizes them.

1 thick slice smoky bacon or pancetta
½ tablespoon olive oil
1 large clove garlic, finely chopped
1 medium red onion, thinly sliced
3 tablespoons chicken stock
2 tablespoons balsamic vinegar
1 ½ quarts mixed piquant leafy greens
   (such as mizuna, arugula, curly endive,
   mustard, etc.) all tough stems removed
salt and freshly ground pepper to taste

GARNISH:
¼ cup toasted pine nuts or walnuts

✤ In a large deep skillet or wok over medium heat, cook bacon or pancetta until crispy. Remove and drain on paper towels. Slice or break into bits and reserve. Add olive oil to bacon drippings in skillet, heat and add garlic and onions. Sauté slowly for 3 to 4 minutes, until softened. Stir in chicken stock and vinegar. Add greens and mix. Stir-fry for 2 to 3 minutes, until leaves are coated. Cover and cook several minutes more, until leaves are wilted and cooked tender-crisp. Top with reserved crisp bacon bits and chopped nuts. Serve hot.

Serves 4

Spicy Stir-Fried Mesclun Salad with Warmed Goat Cheese

A sumptuous, memorable first course for a special dinner celebration.

6 tablespoons olive oil
¼ cup chopped fresh basil
¼ teaspoon freshly ground pepper
Six ½-inch-thick slices goat cheese
   (chèvre)
6 toast rounds, 2 inches in diameter
2 small cloves garlic, minced
2 teaspoons finely chopped fresh ginger
1 small jalapeño chile, seeded and
   chopped very fine
⅓ cup chopped scallions
pinch salt
2 tablespoons orange juice
2 tablespoons balsamic vinegar
3 quarts mesclun salad mix, rinsed and
   drained

✤ Mix together 3 tablespoons oil, basil, and pepper. In a shallow pan, arrange cheese slices and pour oil mixture over. Marinate in refrigerator several hours or overnight.

Preheat over to 400°F. Remove cheese from oil and place on toast. Arrange in small baking pan and bake 5 to 6 minutes until cheese bubbles.

In a wok or deep skillet, heat the remaining 3 tablespoons oil. Add garlic, ginger, chile, scallions, and salt. Stir-fry for 1 minute, until fragrant. Stir in orange juice and vinegar. Add the mesclun, tossing until coated with oil mixture. Cover pan for 1 minute to allow greens to steam through, then remove lid and stir-fry for 30 seconds. Remove immediately to serving platter. Serve on individual plates, topped with toast rounds of warmed goat cheese.

Serves 6

Citrus Chicken Salad with Honey Raspberry Vinaigrette

*Fresh citrus sections combine with juicy chicken in a light
and very delicious herbed raspberry dressing.*

3 chicken breast halves, ½ pound each
2 stalks celery with leaves, chopped
½ medium onion, sliced
1 clove garlic, minced
3 sprigs parsley
½ teaspoon salt
¼ teaspoon pepper

RASPBERRY VINAIGRETTE:
1 tablespoon honey
¼ cup raspberry vinegar
1 clove garlic, minced
1 tablespoon grated onion
1 tablespoon chopped fresh tarragon
½ cup low fat sour cream
½ teaspoon salt

1 pink grapefruit
2 large oranges
½ cup chopped jicama or water chestnuts
3 cups shredded lettuce

GARNISH:
½ cup toasted almonds
2 tablespoons chopped parsley

✦ Place chicken in a medium saucepan with celery, onion, garlic, parsley, salt, and pepper. Add enough water to cover chicken by an inch. Bring to a boil, reduce heat and simmer until chicken is cooked through, about 20 minutes. Turn off heat and let chicken cool in the broth. When cool remove chicken, discard skin and bones, shred meat, and set aside.

Combine ingredients for vinaigrette dressing, mixing until thoroughly blended. Toss dressing gently with shredded chicken.

Cut away peel and pith of grapefruit and oranges and cut free from membranes into sections. Add to chicken along with jicama or water chestnuts. Taste for seasoning. Mound lettuce in center of a large platter. Put orange and grapefruit sections in a circle around the outer edge and mound chicken salad in center. Sprinkle with almonds and chopped parsley and serve.

Serves 4 to 6

Fresh Herb Salad

A salad lover's delight with an explosion of piquant flavors.

DRESSING
2 tablespoons raspberry vinegar
2 tablespoons orange juice
1 teaspoon Dijon mustard
¼ teaspoon salt
¼ teaspoon freshly ground pepper
3 tablespoons olive oil
3 tablespoons salad oil

2 quarts mixed lettuces, torn into bite-
  sized pieces
1 cup loosely packed fresh mint leaves
¼ cup Italian parsley leaves
1 cup loosely packed green basil leaves
¼ cup thinly sliced scallions
2 peaches, peeled and sliced, or 2 cups
  sliced fresh strawberries
⅓ cup toasted chopped hazelnuts

❧ Make the dressing by combining vinegar, orange juice, mustard, salt, and pepper. Gradually add oil, whisking in until thoroughly blended. In a large salad bowl, combine the greens, fruit, and nuts. Pour dressing over salad and toss lightly until coated.

Serves 4 to 6

Millie's Hard-Boiled Egg Salad Dressing

This will remind you of hot summer night suppers in small towns. Wonderful over mixed lettuces, butter lettuce, or as the dressing for coleslaw or potato salad.

1 tablespoon white wine vinegar
1 teaspoon Dijon mustard
¼ teaspoon sugar
2 tablespoons fresh chives, chopped
1 tablespoon fresh parsley, chopped
2 tablespoons fresh dill, chopped
3 tablespoons olive oil
2 tablespoons low-fat sour cream
salt and freshly ground pepper to taste
1 hard boiled egg, finely chopped

❧ Mix together all ingredients except chopped egg. When well blended, stir in egg.

Serves 6

Romaine Lettuce with Sautéed Salad Dressing

1 tablespoon wine vinegar
1 tablespoon lemon juice
1 teaspoon Dijon mustard
¼ cup olive oil
2 large garlic cloves, minced
2 small heads of lettuce, washed and torn
    into bite-size pieces
1 large tomato, seeded, and finely chopped
salt and freshly ground pepper to taste
½ cup toasted chopped walnuts
¼ cup chopped chives
2 tablespoons freshly grated Asiago or
    Parmesan cheese

✢ In a bowl or blender, mix together
vinegar, lemon juice, and mustard. In a
small skillet, heat olive oil. Add garlic
and sauté until just golden, about 2
minutes. Remove from heat. Gradually
whisk in the vinegar mixture, blending
thoroughly. Add salt and pepper to
taste. Arrange lettuce and tomatoes in a
salad bowl. Toss with dressing and
sprinkle walnuts, chives, and cheese
over the top before serving.

Serves 4

Lime Dill Dressing

2 tablespoons lime juice
1 tablespoon vinegar
½ teaspoon sugar
½ teaspoon dry mustard
2 teaspoons coarsely ground dill seed
1 tablespoon mayonnaise
⅓ cup olive oil
salt and freshly ground pepper to taste

✢ Blend together all ingredients except
olive oil, salt, and pepper; add oil in a
steady stream, blending until thoroughly combined. Add salt and pepper
to taste.

Makes about ½ cup

LEMON-CAPER VINAIGRETTE

3 tablespoons freshly squeezed lemon juice
1 clove garlic, minced
2 tablespoons capers, finely chopped
1 tablespoon caper juice
½ cup good fruity olive oil

❖ Combine all ingredients except oil. Add oil slowly, blending well.

Makes ¾ cup

FRESH TOMATO SALAD DRESSING

3 tomatoes, peeled, seeded, and finely chopped
⅓ cup tomato juice
1 clove garlic, finely chopped
2 scallions, including part of green tops, finely chopped
3 tablespoons chopped parsley
½ cup chopped fresh basil
1 tablespoon lemon juice
4 tablespoons red wine vinegar
¼ teaspoon sugar
½ cup olive oil
salt and freshly ground pepper to taste

❖ Combine all ingredients except olive oil, salt, and pepper. Add olive oil in a steady stream, whisking until thoroughly combined. Add salt and pepper to taste.

Makes 1 ½ cups

PESTO SALAD DRESSING

This basil classic is great tossed with green salads, drizzled over a plate of fresh sliced tomatoes, on fresh toasted crusty bread, or over hot fluffy baked potatoes.

1 ½ cups loosely packed fresh basil leaves
½ cup loosely packed flat leaf parsley
½ teaspoon finely chopped fresh oregano
1 clove garlic
½ teaspoon grated lemon zest
2 tablespoons lemon juice
3 tablespoons dry white wine
½ cup freshly grated Parmesan or Asiago cheese
2 tablespoons pine nuts
6 tablespoons fruity olive oil
salt and freshly ground pepper

❖ Combine all the ingredients except salt and pepper in a food processor or blender, processing the mixture until thoroughly blended. Add salt and pepper to taste. Dressing will be thick. Stores well in refrigerator to enjoy over several meals.

Makes 1 cup

GREEK BASIL DRESSING

1 clove garlic, minced
1 shallot or 1 scallion, cut in thirds
6 Greek olives, pitted
1 teaspoon Dijon mustard
1 tablespoon balsamic vinegar
¼ teaspoon grated lemon zest
1 tablespoon fresh lemon juice
1 small tomato, quartered
3 tablespoons chopped fresh basil
¼ teaspoon freshly ground pepper
¼ cup olive oil
salt to taste

❋ In a blender or food processor, blend all ingredients except olive oil and salt. Add olive oil in a steady stream, blending until thoroughly combined. Add salt to taste.

Makes about ⅔ cup

MAX'S RASPBERRY MERLOT VINAIGRETTE

A luxurious, rich-tasting dressing to enjoy with your favorite garden fresh greens. We love it with butter lettuce.

1 large clove garlic, minced
1 shallot, minced
1 teaspoon Dijon mustard
2 teaspoons honey
2 tablespoons raspberry vinegar
⅓ cup Merlot wine
¼ teaspoon salt
¼ teaspoon freshly ground pepper
2 tablespoons olive oil
3 tablespoons vegetable oil
1 cup fresh raspberries or frozen, defrosted and drained
2 tablespoons low-fat sour cream

❋ Combine all ingredients in a food processor or blender, mixing until blended.

Makes 1 ⅓ cups

SESAME SEED SALAD DRESSING

Delicious on butter lettuce; try adding sliced pears or oranges, too.

1 tablespoon balsamic vinegar
1 tablespoon rice vinegar
2 tablespoons orange juice
¼ teaspoon paprika
¼ teaspoon dry mustard
1 teaspoon brown sugar
1 teaspoon soy sauce
3 scallions or 2 shallots, chopped
½ teaspoon sesame oil
6 tablespoons vegetable oil
salt and freshly ground pepper to taste
2 tablespoons toasted sesame seeds

✤ In a bowl combine all ingredients except the oils, sesame seeds, salt, and pepper. Whisk in the oils in a steady stream, mixing until well blended. Add salt and pepper to taste. Just before serving, mix in the sesame seeds.

Makes about ½ cup

BETH'S FRESH SORREL SALAD DRESSING

The combination of lemony sorrel with basil and orange juice makes a scrumptious, light, herbal dressing.

1 large bunch sorrel leaves(about 12 to 15
    large), stems removed, coarsely shredded
5 sprigs fresh basil leaves
½ cup fresh parsley leaves
½ cup olive oil
1 clove garlic, minced
juice of 2 oranges
salt and freshly ground pepper to taste

✤ Combine all the ingredients except salt and pepper in a blender and mix together until liquefied. Add salt and pepper to taste and toss with any fresh lettuce salad.

Makes 1 ⅓ cups

HERBS AND EDIBLE FLOWERS

GREEK-STYLE CHICKEN

Greek olives, fresh herbs and tomatoes, and tangy feta cheese make this dish both colorful and savory.

4 half chicken breast pieces, skinned and boned
3 tablespoons lemon juice
salt and freshly ground pepper to taste
2 tablespoons olive oil
1 tablespoon butter
2 cloves garlic, minced
1 medium onion, chopped
4 tomatoes, peeled, seeded, and coarsely chopped
1 cup dry white wine
2 tablespoons chopped fresh basil
1 teaspoon chopped fresh oregano
¾ cup pitted Greek olives
¼ chopped parsley
⅓ cup crumbled feta cheese
¼ cup chopped parsley

GARNISH:
lemon slices

❉ Sprinkle chicken with 1 tablespoon lemon juice and salt and pepper. Set aside 15 minutes. In a large skillet, heat 1 tablespoon oil and butter. Add chicken and sauté, turning so pieces are lightly browned on both sides. Remove chicken. Add remaining 1 tablespoon of oil to skillet and sauté garlic and onion until softened. Add tomatoes and wine. Bring to a boil, then reduce heat and simmer 5 to 6 minutes until liquid is reduced by half. Return chicken to skillet and add remaining 2 tablespoons lemon juice, basil, oregano, and olives. Simmer until chicken is tender, 4 to 6 minutes. Sprinkle feta cheese over top, and sprinkle with parsley. Taste for seasoning. Garnish with lemon slices and serve.

Serves 4

CLAMS WITH FRESH HERB SAUCE

*Clam lovers will glory in the way this winey herb sauce goes together
with fresh steamed clams.*

2 dozen steamer clams
3 tablespoons of butter
4 cloves garlic, minced
2 shallots, finely chopped
1 tablespoon finely chopped fresh
  lemon thyme
2 teaspoons finely chopped fresh oregano
½ teaspoon finely chopped fresh tarragon
1 teaspoon grated lemon zest
¾ cup dry white wine
⅛ teaspoon ground cayenne pepper
Salt to taste

GARNISH:
⅓ cup chopped parsley
1 lemon, thinly sliced

❧ Scrub clams with a small brush and rinse in cold water.

In a medium skillet, melt butter and sauté garlic and shallots briefly, until translucent, about 3 to 5 minutes. Add herbs, lemon zest, wine, and cayenne pepper and bring to a boil. Reduce heat to medium and cook, stirring, until sauce is reduced by half its volume. This intensifies the sauce and melds flavors. Add salt to taste.

While sauce is cooking, steam clams over rapidly boiling water. Cover pot and steam just until clams open. Immediately remove clams with a slotted spoon or tongs and place in a single layer on a large serving platter and garnish with parsley and lemon slices.

Spoon a portion of the finished sauce over each clam and serve immediately.

Serves 2

BOB'S FABULOUS YUMMY MARINADE

We've enjoyed this wonderfully habit forming marinade-sauce as a marinade for meats, as a sauce for rice or pasta, and as a dressing for green salad. Everyone loves it every which way!

5 tablespoons vegetable oil
⅓ cup packed fresh cilantro with stems
¼ cup fresh lime juice
¼ cup tamari soy sauce
1 ounce fresh ginger, cut into six ¼-inch
   slices
6 large cloves garlic
1 ½ tablespoons ground cumin
1 small, jalapeño or serrano chile pepper

❉ Combine and blend together all ingredients in food processor or blender until the chile, garlic, ginger, and cilantro are finely chopped. Marinade can be made up to 2 days in advance. Bring to room temperature and stir well before using.

Makes 1 ½ cups

DAVE'S GARLIC THYME CHICKEN

The chicken stays moist and tender while becoming infused with the sweet scents of herbs and garlic. A classic light Mediterranean approach that emphasizes flavor and simplicity. Good with fluffy rice to catch the herb-scented juices.

4 half chicken breast pieces, skinned and
   boned
2 tablespoons of fruity olive oil
2 large cloves garlic, minced or mashed
2 tablespoons chopped fresh lemon thyme
2 tablespoons chopped fresh oregano
½ teaspoon freshly ground pepper
½ cup water

❉ For best flavor, prepare chicken pieces several hours in advance. Rub oil well into chicken breasts with your fingers, then rub in the garlic, chopped lemon thyme, oregano, and pepper. Place prepared chicken in heavy skillet, add water, cover and cook over low heat for 10 to 12 minutes, turning once, until chicken is browned on outside and no longer pink in the center. Serve immediately.

Serves 4

HERBED SWORDFISH "BURGERS"

This is a wonderful method for cooking swordfish. The burgers are great with or without buns as a main course.

1 pound swordfish steaks, trimmed and cubed
⅓ large red bell pepper
1 medium onion
2 tablespoons freshly chopped parsley
1 tablespoon freshly chopped dill
1 tablespoon lemon juice
1 tablespoon Dijon mustard
1 tablespoon vegetable oil
salt and freshly ground pepper to taste
bread crumbs

❧ In a food processor, coarsely chop fish, then place in mixing bowl. Process pepper and onion to a fine mince, and add to fish. Add remaining ingredients, using enough bread crumbs to bind. Mixture should be very moist, yet hold together enough to form 4 patties. Size patties to fit rolls, as the burgers will not shrink during cooking. Refrigerate at least ½ hour. Grill over medium coals or cook in a lightly oiled pan, approximately 5 minutes on each side. Serve on buns with lettuce, tomato and Red Pepper Mayonnaise.

Serves 4

RED PEPPER MAYONNAISE

½ cup low-fat mayonnaise
1 tablespoon finely chopped red bell pepper
1 tablespoon chopped chives

❧ Mix together and refrigerate for ½ hour or longer to meld flavors.

Makes ½ cup

CHEESY HERB CRACKERS

*These crisp savory crackers make
delicious snacks or appetizers.*

1 cup flour
½ teaspoon baking powder
½ teaspoon dry mustard
¼ teaspoon salt
¼ cup butter, at room temperature
1 cup finely grated Swiss cheese
¼ cup finely chopped toasted almonds
2 tablespoons finely chopped garlic chives
2 to 3 tablespoons milk

❋ Sift together flour, baking powder,
mustard, and salt. In a medium bowl,
mix together butter and cheese. Add
flour mixture, blending with fingers or
a pastry blender. Mix in almonds and
garlic chives. Add milk 1 tablespoon at a
time, stirring with a fork, until dough
holds together. Shape into a ball, then
press into square log about 1 inch
square by 8 inches long. Wrap in plastic
wrap and chill for several hours.

Preheat oven to 400°F. Slice the
dough into squares about ¼ inch thick
and place them on ungreased baking
sheets. Bake 10 to 12 minutes or until
lightly browned. Cool. Store in tins.

Makes about 3 dozen

CHICKEN MARGARITA

*The tequila and lime juice work magic in
this dish, resulting in the most tender
chicken you've ever tasted!*

1 whole boneless chicken breast, halved

MARINADE:
1 tablespoon oil
¼ cup tequila
juice of 1 fresh lime
½ medium onion, chopped
1 tablespoon chopped garlic
2 tablespoons chopped cilantro
2 tablespoons chopped jalapeño chile
1 teaspoon crushed red pepper flakes

❋ Lay each chicken breast half on a
cutting board and with a sharp knife
slice horizontally, creating a total of
four fillets. Combine marinade ingredients. Place chicken in marinade, cover,
and refrigerate for 4 hours, turning
often. Grill over medium coals until no
longer pink inside.

Serves 2

HERBED RICE TORTE

A satisfying side dish or main event.

1 tablespoon butter
2 tablespoons olive oil
1 clove garlic, minced
1 large onion, finely chopped
1 cup Arborio or other short-grain
   white rice
1 cup white wine
2 to 2 ½ cups chicken stock
½ cup chopped fresh basil
salt and freshly ground pepper to taste

TOPPING:
3 tablespoons freshly grated Parmesan
   cheese
2 tablespoons bread crumbs
1 tablespoon butter

❄ Preheat oven to 350°F. In a 3- to 4-quart saucepan, heat 1 tablespoon butter and olive oil over high heat. Add garlic and onion and sauté until softened. Add rice and stir about 3 minutes, until rice is well coated and no longer transparent. Add wine, stirring constantly until it boils, then add 2 cups of the chicken stock. Return to a boil then reduce heat and simmer uncovered until liquid has been absorbed, about 25 to 30 minutes. Stir frequently toward the end of cooking time to prevent sticking, adding more stock if rice is too firm. Stir in basil and salt and pepper to taste. Spoon rice into a greased 9-inch pie plate or springform pan.

Combine Parmesan and bread crumbs. Sprinkle over top of rice. Dot with remaining 1 tablespoon butter.

Bake torte for 20 to 25 minutes, until thoroughly heated. Cut into wedges and serve.

Serves 6 to 8

Pesto Bread Crumbs

Great on cooked veggies or deviled eggs, or to top casseroles.

1 cup dry bread crumbs
2 large cloves garlic, chopped
¼ cup freshly grated Parmesan or Asiago cheese
3 tablespoons toasted pine nuts
1 ½ cups loosely packed fresh basil leaves
¼ teaspoon salt
⅛ teaspoon freshly ground pepper

✤ Combine all ingredients in a food processor until thoroughly blended. After using, refrigerate any leftovers.

Makes 2 cups

Pronto Pesto Pasta

If you are a confirmed pesto lover, here's a surefire way to make it without undue ceremony on a busy summer night.

✤ 1 day before: cut a large peeled halved garlic clove in half and combine with 4 to 6 tablespoons good fruity olive oil. (Refrigerate if made more than 1 day in advance, but don't store over 1 week.)

20 minutes before dinner: Put a big pot of water on to boil for pasta. With a good chopping knife or cleaver, very finely chop together 2 cups fresh basil leaves and ½ cup fresh parsley. Add 1 cup toasted pine nuts, 1 ½ cups freshly grated Asiago or Parmesan cheese, ½ teaspoon salt and pepper to taste. Remove and discard the garlic clove from premade garlic oil and add oil to mixture. Mix well.

Cook and drain 12 ounces linguine. Combine with basil-cheese mixture and toss well with 2 big forks. Serve immediately and enjoy immensely!

Serves 4

Dilled Brittle Bread Crisps

A wonderful light and crunchy herbed cracker bread to serve with wine or juice anytime.

2 ¾ cups flour (plus flour to roll dough in)
2 tablespoons sugar
¾ teaspoon salt
½ teaspoon baking soda
2 tablespoons coarsely ground dill seeds
¼ pound butter
1 cup fresh plain yogurt

EGG WASH:
1 egg, beaten with 1 teaspoon water

whole dill seeds
coarse salt

Preheat oven to 450°F. In a food processor or with a pastry blender, combine 2 ¾ cups flour, sugar, salt, baking soda, and dill seeds. Add butter and process until mixture is like a coarse meal. Add yogurt and mix until just combined. Make into small balls the size of almonds. Refrigerate until chilled. On a lightly floured board roll each ball out as thin as possible. Place on an ungreased baking sheet. Brush with egg wash, sprinkle generously with whole dill seeds and coarse salt.

Bake 5 minutes or until golden brown in upper part of oven. Remove from pan to cool. Store in tin box or sealed container.

Makes 4 to 5 dozen

Creamy Sorrel Sauce

A wonderful sauce for fresh grilled salmon, halibut, or sea bass.

½ cup very fresh plain yogurt
½ cup low fat mayonnaise
1 cup fresh sorrel (approximately 10 to 11 leaves), stems removed, leaves chopped
1 tablespoon soy sauce
1 small clove garlic, finely chopped
dash of cayenne pepper

In a food processor or blender, blend all ingredients together thoroughly.

Makes 1 ½ cups

Chive Butter for Grilled Corn

1 stick (¼ pound) butter, softened
1 teaspoon fresh lemon juice
2 tablespoons chopped fresh chives
¼ teaspoon freshly ground pepper

Mix lemon juice, chives, and pepper into butter and serve with corn grilled in its husks.

Rosy Caraway Cheese Dip

Pumpernickel or other dark bread goes along well with this savory dip.

8 ounces low fat cream cheese, at room
  temperature
1 tablespoon butter, at room temperature
1 tablespoon Dijon mustard
1 large shallot, minced
4 teaspoons caraway seeds
4 teaspoons paprika
4 teaspoons capers, drained

GARNISH:
 2 tablespoons chopped chives

❧ In a food processor or a bowl combine all ingredients except capers and chives. Process or mix until very well blended. Add capers and blend in for a few seconds. Chill. Serve in a bowl sprinkled with chives. Best if made several days ahead.

Makes about 1 cup

Fresh Salmon with Tricolored Peppercorn Sauce

Elegant, simple, and sure to draw raves!

½ lemon
salmon steaks or fillets to serve 4
2 ½ tablespoons butter (don't substitute)
1 teaspoon Dijon mustard
1 teaspoon fresh lemon juice
1 tablespoon finely crushed tricolored
  peppercorns

❧ Squeeze juice from lemon half over salmon and barbecue or broil salmon— don't overcook. Melt butter, mixing in mustard and lemon juice. When salmon fillets are done, sprinkle crushed peppercorns evenly over them, then drizzle melted butter sauce over everything. Serve immediately.

Serves 4

SPICE LOVERS' GLAZED MEATBALLS

1 pound ground lean beef or turkey
¼ pound bulk pork sausage
2 tablespoons tomato juice
2 tablespoons soy sauce
1 egg, lightly beaten
¼ cup dry bread crumbs
¼ cup thinly sliced scallions
⅓ cup coarsely chopped water chestnuts
¼ teaspoon salt
¼ teaspoon freshly ground pepper
¼ teaspoon allspice
¼ teaspoon ginger
½ teaspoon dry mustard
1 ½ teaspoons crushed coriander seeds

GLAZE:
⅔ cup apple jelly
⅔ cup Major Grey's chutney, finely
   chopped
1 tablespoon lemon juice

✤ In a bowl combine meats, tomato juice, soy sauce, egg, bread crumbs, scallions, water chestnuts, and spices. Shape into 1-inch balls. Place on a baking sheet and refrigerate 30 minutes.

Preheat oven to 450°F. Bake meatballs uncovered for 15 minutes or until browned. Drain off excess juice.

In a large skillet, combine glaze ingredients and heat until melted. Add meatballs, cover, and cook over low heat 5 to 10 minutes until glazed. Serve hot.

Makes 3 ½ dozen

HERBED TRICOLORED PEPPERCORN CHEESE BALL

8 ounces low fat cream cheese, at room
   temperature
1 small clove garlic, minced
1 teaspoon caraway seed, crushed
¼ cup finely chopped chives
2 tablespoons chopped dill leaf
1 teaspoon Worcestershire sauce
1 tablespoon tricolor peppercorns, ground
   fine in a blender

GARNISH:
1 teaspoon finely chopped parsley

✤ Mix together all ingredients except peppercorns and parsley and form into a ball. Chill in refrigerator for 20 minutes. Remove and roll in ground peppercorns. Garnish by sprinkling chopped parsley over top. Serve with crispy crackers.

Makes 1 cheese ball (about 1 ¼ cups)

LEMON THYME PESTO

Delicious spread on baguette slices or on baked potatoes, cooked carrots, rice, pasta and tomato slices—indeed, it's good on almost everything!

⅔ cup chopped lemon thyme leaves
⅔ cup lightly toasted almonds
½ cup freshly grated Parmesan cheese
⅛ teaspoon freshly ground pepper
1 clove garlic, minced
1 tablespoon fresh lemon juice
4 to 5 tablespoons olive oil

✢ Blend all ingredients in food processor or blender, making into a rough paste. Store in refrigerator until ready to serve, up to 1 week.

Makes approximately 1 cup

LEMON THYME BARBECUE SAUCE

This versatile sauce is easy to make. Enjoy it over grilled chicken or fish, or spoon over freshly baked or boiled potatoes.

3 tablespoons white wine vinegar
1 tablespoon fresh lemon juice
2 teaspoons Dijon mustard
1 shallot, minced
6 scallions, white part only, chopped
2 tablespoons chopped fresh lemon thyme
¼ cup chopped fresh parsley
3 tablespoons vegetable oil
3 tablespoons olive oil
¼ teaspoon paprika
salt and freshly ground pepper to taste

✢ Combine all ingredients except salt and pepper. Let flavor develop for ½ hour before using. Add salt and pepper to taste.

Makes ¾ cup

LEMON THYME BUTTERMILK BISCUITS

These light, herb scented biscuits make delicious breakfast or brunch fare to serve with scrambled eggs. They are also elegant paired with poached salmon.

2 cups flour
2 teaspoons baking powder
1 teaspoon baking soda
½ teaspoon salt
1 teaspoon sugar
3 tablespoons chilled butter, cut into small pieces
⅓ cup vegetable shortening
3 tablespoons chopped lemon thyme
¼ cup chopped chives
¾ cup plus 1 tablespoon buttermilk

❉ Preheat oven to 425°F. Lightly grease a 9-inch square baking pan. Sift together flour, baking powder, baking soda, salt, and sugar into a bowl. With a pastry blender or fingertips, cut or rub butter and shortening into dry ingredients until the mixture has the consistency of coarse crumbs. Blend in lemon thyme and chives. Add ¾ cup of buttermilk all at once, and stir with a fork until the dough just comes together.

Turn dough out onto a lightly floured pastry cloth or board. Shape into a ball, then knead lightly about 5 to 6 times. Pat or roll out dough to about ½-inch thickness. Using a floured 2-inch biscuit cutter or the rim of a glass, cut dough into 12 or more biscuits. Arrange biscuits in pan so they are just touching each other. Brush tops with remaining 1 tablespoon of buttermilk. Bake 15 to 18 minutes until fluffy and golden brown.

Makes 12 to 16

ORANGE POPPY SEED CAKE

1 cup flour, sifted
1 teaspoon baking powder
¼ teaspoon salt
2 eggs, at room temperature
1 cup sugar
1 teaspoon grated orange zest
1 teaspoon Grand Marnier or other orange
  liqueur
¼ cup poppy seeds
1 tablespoon butter
½ cup hot milk

SYRUP TOPPING:
juice of 1 orange
juice of ½ lemon
⅓ cup sugar

Powdered sugar for dusting (optional)

❧ Preheat oven to 350°F. Lightly grease and flour an 8- or 9-inch cake or springform pan. Sift together flour, baking powder, and salt three times and leave in sifter; set aside.

In the large bowl of an electric mixer, beat eggs for 3 to 4 minutes until thick and lemon-colored. Gradually add 1 cup sugar and beat for another 5 minutes. Add the orange zest, orange liqueur, and poppy seeds, mixing until combined.

Melt the butter in hot milk. Using a rubber spatula, mix the hot milk into the egg mixture all at once. Sift the flour into the mixture, gradually folding it in. (The folding in of the milk and dry ingredients should take only about 1 minute. The batter will be thin.) Pour batter into prepared pan. Bake for 25 to 35 minutes or until a cake tester inserted in center of cake comes out clean.

While cake is baking, prepare syrup topping. In a small saucepan, mix the juices with sugar. Heat, stirring until sugar dissolves, then simmer for 5 minutes. Transfer cake to a rack. Poke top of cake repeatedly with a fork. Spoon warm topping over cake. Cool completely. If making ahead, wrap cake in plastic wrap and chill in refrigerator. Just before serving sprinkle with powdered sugar, if desired.

Serves 8 to 10

Cinnamon Basil Cookies

2 cups flour
½ teaspoon baking soda
½ teaspoon cinnamon
¼ teaspoon salt
¾ cup butter at room temperature
¾ cup sugar
1 egg
¼ cup chopped fresh cinnamon basil
½ cup finely chopped walnuts

TOPPING:
3 tablespoons sugar
2 teaspoons cinnamon

❋ Sift together the flour, baking soda, ½ teaspoon cinnamon, and salt. Set aside. In a bowl cream the butter with ¾ cup sugar until light and fluffy. Beat in the egg, mixing until combined. Stir in cinnamon, basil, dry ingredients, and nuts, blending thoroughly. Wrap and chill the dough for 1 hour or until firm. Meanwhile, preheat oven to 350°F.

Shape the dough into 1-inch balls. Combine remaining 3 tablespoons sugar and 2 teaspoons cinnamon. Roll the balls of dough in this mixture until coated. Place 2 inches apart on ungreased baking sheets. Press cookies down with the palm of hand to flatten them slightly. Bake 10 to 12 minutes or until golden. Transfer to racks to cool.

Makes about 5 dozen

Spiced Pears with Zinfandel and Cinnamon Basil

A beautiful, not-too-sweet dessert; the pears take on a rosy hue and a subtle cinnamon basil fragrance.

POACHING LIQUID:
1 bottle (750 ml) Beaujolais, Zinfandel, or other fruity, full flavored red wine
1 cup sugar
6 sprigs cinnamon basil (stems and leaves)
1 two-to three-inch strip of fresh orange peel
2 cinnamon sticks

6 firm pears (Bartlett, Bosc, or Anjou)

GARNISH:
Cinnamon basil leaves and flowers

❋ In a large skillet, heat wine, sugar, basil sprigs, orange peel, and cinnamon sticks. Bring to a boil, then reduce heat and simmer 5 minutes.

Peel, halve, and core pears. Lay pears cut side down in poaching liquid. Simmer 15 minutes, then with a wooden spoon turn pears over and poach an additional 5 minutes or until tender but still firm. Place pears in a shallow dish to cool, immersed in the juice. Chill until serving time. Serve pears in individual bowls. Spoon some of poaching liquid over each pear, and garnish with fresh cinnamon basil leaves.

Serves 6

LEMON BASIL SNAPS WITH PISTACHIO NUTS

2 cups flour
½ teaspoon baking soda
¼ teaspoon salt
¾ cup butter, at room temperature
¾ cup sugar
1 egg
1 tablespoon grated lemon zest
1 tablespoon lemon juice
⅓ cup chopped fresh lemon basil

TOPPING:
⅓ cup finely chopped pistachio nuts
3 tablespoons sugar

❋ Sift together the flour, baking soda, and salt. Set aside. In a bowl cream the butter and sugar until light and fluffy. Beat in the egg, mixing until combined. Add lemon zest, lemon juice, and lemon basil. Stir in the dry ingredients, blending thoroughly. Wrap and chill the dough for 1 hour or until firm. Meanwhile, preheat oven to 350°F.

Shape the dough into 1-inch balls. Combine nuts with 3 tablespoons sugar. Roll the balls of dough in sugar-nut mixture until coated. Place 2 inches apart on ungreased baking sheets. Flatten cookies slightly with the palm of hand. Bake 10 to 12 minutes or until golden. Transfer to racks to cool.

Makes about 5 dozen

PAOLA'S FRESH PEAR COFFEE CAKE WITH CINNAMON OR ANISE BASIL

2 cups diced soft ripe pears
⅓ finely chopped anise or cinnamon basil
  leaves
1 cup flour, sifted
1 teaspoon baking soda
½ teaspoon cinnamon
⅛ teaspoon nutmeg (freshly grated if
  possible)
¼ teaspoon salt
1 cup sugar
¼ cup vegetable oil
1 egg, lightly beaten
½ teaspoon vanilla extract
½ cup chopped walnuts or almonds

❋ Preheat oven to 375°F. Grease and flower a 8 x 8 x 2-inch pan. Toss pears with basil. Set aside. Sift together the flour, baking soda, cinnamon, nutmeg, and salt. In a separate bowl mix sugar and vegetable oil. Add beaten egg and vanilla, mixing until thoroughly combined. Add dry ingredients, mixing until just blended. Mix in pears and nuts. Mixture will be very thick—mix quickly. Spoon into baking pan. Bake 25 minutes, then lower heat to 325°F and bake 30 minutes longer or until a cake tester comes out clean.

Serves 6 to 8

CINNAMON BASIL FRUIT TORTE

The tender crisp crust and light fruit filling are enhanced by the unique cinnamon basil flavor and delectable meringue topping.

PASTRY:
1 cup flour
½ teaspoon baking powder
¼ teaspoon salt
⅓ cup firmly packed light brown sugar
⅓ cup butter
1 egg yolk
1 teaspoon grated lemon zest
1 tablespoon fresh lemon juice

FRUIT FILLING:
3 cups thinly sliced ripe nectarines or
   (peeled) peaches
1 tablespoon flour
¼ cup granulated sugar
⅓ cup finely chopped cinnamon basil

MERINGUE TOPPING:
2 egg whites, at room temperature
⅛ teaspoon salt
⅓ cup firmly packed light brown sugar
¼ cup finely chopped almonds
dash cinnamon

❊ Preheat oven to 325°F. Lightly grease an 8 x 11-inch baking pan.

Pastry: In a mixing bowl combine flour, baking powder, salt, and brown sugar. Mash butter into flour with fingers or a fork until mixture is like cornmeal. Mix egg yolk, lemon zest, and juice and add to the flour mixture, stirring with a fork until blended. (Add a few drops of water if pastry doesn't hold together.) Press pastry into pan, shaping it ½ inch up the sides of the pan. Bake 12 minutes. Cool 10 minutes.

Combine fruit with flour, granulated sugar, and cinnamon basil. Pour off any excess juice, then arrange fruit slices over pastry. Whisk egg whites until frothy, add salt, and whisk until egg whites are stiff but not dry. Mix in brown sugar. Spread meringue over fruit, sprinkle with almonds, and dust with cinnamon. Bake 35 minutes. Serve immediately.

Serves 8

RHUBARB PEAR CRUNCH SCENTED WITH ROSE GERANIUMS

A velvety and delicious warm dessert with an exotic flavor hint of roses to tantalize your taste. Serve warm with vanilla ice cream.

2 teaspoons orange zest
¼ cup orange juice
2 tablespoons finely chopped rose scented geranium leaves
1 ½ pounds (about 4 cups) fresh rhubarb, cut into 1-inch pieces
3 firm, ripe pears, peeled, cored, and cut into 1-inch chunks
½ cup sugar
2 tablespoons cornstarch
¼ teaspoon cinnamon

TOPPING:
½ cup flour
½ cup firmly packed brown sugar
¼ teaspoon allspice
¾ cup rolled oats (not quick-cooking)
¼ cup butter, at room temperature
½ cup chopped toasted walnuts

✣ Set orange zest aside. In a saucepan, heat orange juice with geranium leaves just until warm. Cover and set aside to steep for 15 minutes.

Preheat oven to 350°F. Lightly grease a 9-inch square baking pan or a 1 ½- to 2-quart baking dish. Place rhubarb and pears in a bowl. Toss with orange zest and geranium-steeped orange juice. In a small bowl, combine sugar, cornstarch, and cinnamon. Add to fruit, tossing well to combine. Spoon into baking dish.

Combine flour, brown sugar, allspice, and rolled oats. With your fingertips, rub butter into dry ingredients until the mixture resembles a coarse meal. Stir in walnuts. Spread topping over fruit, patting it down gently.

Bake 50 to 60 minutes, or until bubbly and brown.

Serves 6

ROSE SCENTED GERANIUM SUGAR

Easy to make, this fragrant sugar goes well in iced or hot tea, lemonade, or punch. It is delicious sprinkled over sugar cookies, shortbread, or mix it with sour cream or fresh yogurt to top fresh berries, or use it to make a floral icing for your favorite cake.

*l large handful rose scented geranium
  leaves*
4 cups sugar

❋ Wash and thoroughly dry geranium leaves, then bruise them between the palms of your hands. Pour ½ cup sugar into a 4-cup mason jar, and place a layer of leaves on top. Add another ½ cup sugar, then another layer of leaves. Continue in this manner until jar is full. Cap tightly, and let flavors infuse for a week before using.

ROSE GERANIUM BUTTER FOR BREAKFAST BISCUITS

Because this is a sweet butter, it goes particularly well with jam and biscuits. But substitute parsley, chervil, sweet marjoram, or lemon thyme for the rose geranium and the butter is equally delicious over steamed vegetables.

*½ cup unsalted butter, at room
  temperature*
*1 tablespoon minced rose scented
  geranium leaves*
1 teaspoon grated orange zest

❋ Combine all ingredients in a small mixing bowl. With the back of a wooden spoon work geranium leaves and zest into butter until well combined. Chill butter for about 10 minutes, then place it on a sheet of plastic wrap. Roll butter into a cylinder about the width of a half-dollar. Wrap and refrigerate, then use as needed.

POACHED CHICKEN BREASTS WITH JULIENNED ROOT VEGETABLES

A flavorful and quick fall meal that looks beautiful and tastes moist and delicious.

POACHING LIQUID:
3 tablespoons olive oil
½ onion, finely chopped
⅓ cup dry white wine
⅓ cup chicken stock
1 leafy sprig of dill, 3 to 4 inches long

4 large chicken breasts, halved, skinned,
  and boned

MIX TOGETHER WELL:
1 large carrot, cut into fine julienned strips
1 parsnip, cut into fine julienned strips
1 stalk celery, cut into fine julienned strips
1 red bell pepper, cut into fine julienned
  strips

GARNISH:
2 tablespoons chopped fresh parsley

❖ To make poaching liquid, in a small saucepan heat 2 teaspoons of the olive oil. Add onion and sauté until tender, about 3 minutes. Pour in wine and chicken stock, stirring to combine, then add dill sprig. Bring to a boil. Cover and simmer for 2 minutes. Set aside.

To prepare chicken, sprinkle both sides of chicken breasts lightly with salt and pepper. In a 10 inch skillet, heat 1 more tablespoon of oil quickly and brown one side of each chicken breast and add to poaching liquid. Top each breast with a generous amount of the julienned vegetable mixture. Cover and poach gently until breasts are tender and flesh is no longer pink inside (approximately 10 to 15 minutes). Place on serving plate and spoon a bit of poaching liquid over breasts Sprinkle with salt and pepper to taste. Garnish with chopped parsley.

Serves 4

EDIBLE FLOWERS

ANISE HYSSOP WALNUT COOKIES

A new turn on a traditional English tea cookie. These thin cookies will delight lovers of anise's delicate flavor.

1 cup chopped walnuts
1 cup firmly packed light brown sugar
¼ cup flour
¼ teaspoon salt
½ teaspoon anise seeds
2 eggs, lightly beaten
3 tablespoons chopped anise hyssop leaves

❀ Preheat oven to 375°F. In a food processor or blender, combine walnuts, sugar, flour, salt, and anise seeds. Process until walnuts are finely ground. Thoroughly mix with eggs and chopped anise hyssop. Drop dough by rounded teaspoonfuls on a well-greased baking sheet, spacing cookies 2 inches apart. Bake about 8 minutes or until edges are golden brown. Remove to a rack to cool.

Makes about 30 cookies

MELON WITH LAVENDER SYRUP

Join us in reviving the old-fashioned art of cooking with aromatic lavender.

½ cup sugar
½ cup water
¼ cup sweet dessert wine (Sauternes, Grenache, or sweet Riesling)
2 tablespoons orange juice
¼ cup fresh or dried lavender flowers
1 large ripe melon, cut into cubes (using any sweet ripe variety)

GARNISH:
fresh mint leaves

❀ Bring sugar, water, wine, and orange juice to a boil, reduce heat, and simmer 5 minutes, stirring once or twice to dissolve sugar. Add lavender flowers. Remove from heat, cover and steep 1 to 2 hours. Strain out lavender flowers, pressing on pulp. To serve, pour syrup over melon, gently toss. Garnish with mint leaves.

Serves 4 to 6

PEACH COFFEE CAKE WITH ANISE HYSSOP

The delicate sweet flavor of anise hyssop flowers softly scents this pretty and not overly sweet fruit coffee cake. Perfect fare for your afternoon coffee or tea break!

5 peaches, peeled and sliced
2 teaspoons lemon juice
½ cup plus 1 tablespoon sugar
3 ½ tablespoons chopped anise hyssop leaves and blossoms
1 cup flour
¾ teaspoon baking powder
¼ teaspoon salt
¼ teaspoon ground anise seed
½ cup butter
2 eggs
1 teaspoon vanilla extract

TOPPING:
¼ cup chopped almonds mixed with 3 tablespoons sugar

✣ Preheat oven to 350°F. Lightly grease a 9-inch flan or springform pan with a removable bottom. In a bowl combine peaches, lemon juice, the 1 tablespoon sugar, and 2 tablespoons anise hyssop. Set aside.

Sift together flour, baking powder, salt, and ground anise. In a bowl, cream butter and remaining ½ cup sugar until fluffy. Add eggs, one at a time, mixing until thoroughly blended. Stir in the remaining 1 ½ tablespoons anise hyssop and vanilla. Stir in dry ingredients, mixing just until combined. Spread batter into prepared pan. Pour off any excess juice from peaches, then arrange slices in concentric circles on top of batter. Sprinkle with almond and sugar mixture. Bake for 1 hour until golden brown. If fruit is very juicy spoon off excess liquid while it is baking.

Serves 8

LAVENDER SHORTBREAD

A lovely rich shortbread with a hint of sweet lavender fragrance and flavor. Perfect to serve with tea in the afternoon.

1 ½ cups (¾ pound) butter, at room
   temperature (no substitutes)
⅔ cup sugar
2 tablespoons finely chopped lavender
   florets
1 tablespoon chopped fresh mint
2 ⅓ cups flour
½ cup cornstarch
¼ teaspoon salt

GARNISH:
lavender powdered sugar: Put a few
   lavender flowers in a sealed jar with
   powdered sugar for a day before using
   sugar.

❋ Preheat oven to 325°F. Cover bottoms of two baking sheets with parchment or brown paper.

In a large bowl, cream together the butter, sugar, lavender, and mint with an electric mixer. Mix until light and fluffy, about 3 minutes. Add flour, cornstarch, and salt and beat until incorporated. Divide dough in half. Flatten into squares and wrap in plastic. Chill until firm.

On a floured board, roll or pat out each square to a thickness of ½ inch. Cut the dough into 1 ½-inch squares or rounds. Transfer to baking sheets, spacing cookies about 1 inch apart. Prick each cookie several times with the tines of a fork. Bake 20 to 25 minutes until pale golden (do not brown). Cool slightly, then transfer to a rack. Sprinkle with lavender powdered sugar. Store in tin cookie boxes or sealed containers.

Makes about 4 dozen

CRYSTALLIZED PETITE VIOLAS

A lovely, old-fashioned way to decorate cakes, custards, and puddings.

1 cup fresh viola flowers, gently rinsed and patted dry
1 egg white, at room temperature
¼ cup superfine sugar

✣ Beat egg white until frothy. With a small, clean, art or pastry brush, coat all sides of each flower's petals with beaten egg white gently and completely. Sprinkle flowers carefully and completely with sugar. Place on a cake rack over a baking sheet and let dry thoroughly in a cool dry place.

Store in a covered airtight container until ready to use.

SOME FAVORITE EDIBLE FLOWER USES

✣ As a garnish in fruit, salads, and drinks, try anise hyssop, borage, lavender, or johnny jump-up flowers.

✣ In appetizers and green salads, use johnny jump-ups, violas, chive blossoms, calendulas, or nasturtiums.

✣ In potato salads, use nasturtiums, chive blossoms, gem marigolds, or blue borage flowers.

✣ Add calendula petals to scrambled eggs and cheese omelets.

✣ Mix nasturtium petals into any savory sandwich filling, or use in shrimp salads or to decorate fresh pasta salad, or in hot pasta primavera.

✣ Freeze anise hyssop, johnny jump-up, viola, or borage flowers in ice cubes to add to iced tea.

Caution: not all flowers are edible. Pick and use only those you have personally verified to be edible from an authoritative souce. Use only blossoms you are certain have not been sprayed, as most chemicals registered strictly for ornamentals are toxic.

INDEX

Fresh from Ten Speed Press

RECIPES FROM A KITCHEN GARDEN
by Renee Shepherd and Fran Raboff

There's nothing quite like the taste of your own home-grown produce, fresh from the garden. But even if your bounty comes fresh from the store, this delightful collection of over 300 recipes will inspire you with ideas for cooking with vegetables, fragrant herbs, and edible flowers. From the proprietor of Shepherd's Garden Seeds, one of the largest specialty seed companies in the country, this bumper crop of recipes will create a delicious, nutritious feast at your table.

THE KITCHEN GARDENER'S GUIDE
edited by Donald Berg

Not that long ago, every homemaker depended on a kitchen garden for fresh fruits and vegetables all year round. The time-tested secrets in this book will allow anyone to plan, seed, grow, and harvest a bounty for the table.

THE AFTER-DINNER GARDENING BOOK
by Richard W. Langer

A guide to using window boxes, window sills, and even coffee cans on tables to grow a steady supply of fresh, interesting produce—using the seeds from food you eat every day.

LAZY BED GARDENING
by John Jeavons & Dave Smith

This "quick and dirty guide" distills the essentials of biointensive gardening for those who don't have the time or inclination to put in a lot of effort. Based on HOW TO GROW MORE VEGETABLES, it focuses on simple techniques for getting started on a small, easy to maintain, but highly productive garden.

Available from your local bookstore, or order direct from the publisher. For more information, write for our free complete catalog of over 500 books, posters, and tapes.

Ten Speed Press
Box 7123
Berkeley, CA 94707